WILDNESS
AND BEING HUMAN

WILDNESS
AND BEING HUMAN

by

Walt McLaughlin

Wood Thrush Books

Cover image: Cave paintings of Altamira, photographed by Julio
Merencio Ricote, courtesy of Shutterstock.com.

Published by Wood Thrush Books
            27 Maple Grove Estates
            Swanton, Vermont 05488

ISBN 978-1-7345175-5-2

Acknowledgements

While there are many people who have assisted me during my exploration of human nature and the writing of this book, I must acknowledge two in particular. Rob Faivre provided me with invaluable resources in the fields of anthropology and sociology. My depiction of humankind's earliest cultural development would have been sorely lacking without his input. Benjamin Green read the first few chapters of this book while it was still in an intermediate draft. He brought to my attention its stylistic flaws, helping me set the proper tone. To both men I am grateful.

Then there is my wife Judy, who put up with my blathering while I was researching and writing this book. Her patience in this regard is always remarkable, as long as I don't assault her with my thoughts before nine o'clock in the morning.

Contents

I wish to speak a word for Nature, for absolute freedom and wildness, as contrasted with a freedom and culture merely civil – to regard man as an inhabitant, or a part and parcel of Nature, rather than a member of society.

– Henry David Thoreau

WILDNESS
AND BEING HUMAN

1. Going Feral

Winter loosens its grip on the mountains. I tramp a muddy, unimproved road reaching back into a high valley until I come to a beaten path veering into the woods. I stop to catch my breath before following the path down to a brook raging with snowmelt. The path fades to a game trail that gradually disappears. That's when I feel the first surge of wildness rise from somewhere deep within. While bushwhacking along the stream, dodging saplings, branches and downed trees, with cold mud squishing underfoot and lingering patches of snow all around, I reconnect with my primal self. Suddenly that life of mine back in the developed lowlands no longer defines me. Not completely, anyhow. Now I am something else, as well – a cognizant, bipedal creature with roots deep in the natural world.

I wipe away sweat beading on my brow despite a chill in the air. The nearby brook is all whitewater crashing over rocks, fed by countless runoff streams. Evergreen wood ferns, still pressed firmly to the ground, foreshadow the growing season ahead. That is comforting. I caress a patch of soft, wet moss covering a huge boulder as shafts of sunlight break through the clouds gathering overhead. Then I traverse a mudslide dropping sharply to the brook. My boot slips on a half-frozen patch of sloped earth and down I go. I laugh away the pain while scrambling back to my feet. Now one side of me is cold, wet and muddy. Nature is raw and unforgiving in early spring. I love her all the same.

Once I have gone a mile or so upstream, I drop to my knees along the edge of the brook and splash ice cold water into my face. It drips from my beard while I'm looking around, admiring the stolid hemlocks, birches, beeches and maples – the way they plant themselves in the soil and reach towards the sky as if nothing matters more than existence. I catch a whiff of decomposed leaves then lean back against a large, smooth rock and let the wild slowly consume me. And the stream, endlessly flowing downhill, washes away any remnant sense of self-importance that I still harbor as a member of the human race.

I am a civilized man. I was born and raised in cities and small towns, and have lived most of my life in the developed lowlands. I have spent the vast majority of my time immersed in the modern, manmade world. I work and play on electronic devices that are marvels of human innovation. I am literate, steeped in the arts, and well educated. I do my best to be polite in social settings, drive safely, and am a law-abiding citizen for the most part. From all outward appearances, I am as far removed from the harsh, survival-of-the-fittest realities of wild nature as anyone can be. Yet I feel the most like myself whenever I'm alone in a wild forest, wandering about aimlessly. Why is this? What is it about nature that makes me feel so comfortable in my skin? What is it about me, as a human being, that makes it so easy to feel at home in the wild, yet so profoundly alienated by the complex systems and never-ending machinations of my own kind?

I realize I'm something of an oddball. Whenever I say to my wife that I feel perfectly normal, she bursts into laughter. That usually brings me back to my senses. Granted, most people don't enjoy wandering aimlessly in the woods alone, or pondering philosophical matters as much as I do. Still I can't help but think that wandering and pondering are traits common to all human beings. Much of our deep past indicates this, as does the more recent history of our migrations, explorations, creations, and discoveries. We have been wandering as long as we have been bipedal. We have been pondering as long as we have had the gray matter to do so. All this leads me to believe that the tension I feel between my wild and civilized selves is universal, that the difference between one person and another in this regard is only a matter of degree. If this is the case, then there's something terribly wrong with the way we have organized ourselves through the millennia, as well as the way we live our lives today.

Relaxed, happy and a little fatigued, I make my way back to the unimproved road then exit the woods. My work awaits me, as do the many obligations I have back in the developed lowlands. I fire up the engine of my car and commence the long drive home. Only a few miles down the paved road, even though I'm going much faster than it seems natural to go, there is soon a car on my tail, then two, then several more. I pull over to let them all pass, allowing their drivers to get on with their busy lives at the frenzied pace that is now considered normal. Eventually I get back into the swing of things, blasting down the interstate several miles above the speed limit. Still I'm being passed.

Soon I am back home yet longing to be in the woods again. Next time for a couple days, maybe more. And that's how I as a civilized man cultivate my wildness without even trying. Repeated exposure to the wild makes me want more of it. Leave a domesticated cat outdoors long enough and there's a good chance it will go feral. This must be true about some human beings, as well.

How much of me is wild? How much is domesticated? It's hard to say to what extent any human being is one or the other. Because we are thinking creatures, our domestication is more a state of mind than an irreversible condition. In fact everything about the domesticating, *civilizing* process, which began for each of us when we were young children, is designed to keep wildness at bay, or at least sublimate it. Art is a good example of this sublimation, along with any kind of innovation. What creative endeavor doesn't have an element of wildness in it? But that's where the matter gets tricky. When is it okay to go wild? When is it not okay? And who's making the rules to determine this, anyhow? The wild mind is a creative mind, an innovative mind, but it is also revolutionary. The wild mind is a threat to the status quo because it is naturally rule breaking. Yes indeed, wildness versus domestication is a tricky matter.

As someone who has wandered the woods and thought creatively for decades, I have allowed my own wildness to get a little out of hand. I have cultivated it to the extent that I now find it difficult to function within the straightjacket of civilization. I keep my wildness in check by sheer force of will, but every once in a while I find myself raging against the machine. I am not alone in this regard. I have met others who also feel alienated from modern society. They express their alienation through deviant behavior, extreme political views, dropping out, or simply being an outsider one way or another.

There are innumerable tensions in modern society between individuals and institutions, between different groups, between one person and another. I suspect that most, if not all, of these tensions can be traced back to the tension between the all-too-human urge to wildness and the trappings of domesticated life that inhibit our basic desire to wander and ponder freely. Whenever I let myself go feral, if only for a day, it becomes clear to me right away where the problem lies. The various social structures that we have created to make life easier for ourselves constrain our fundamentally wild human nature. In other words, we have not organized ourselves well. Civilization is, at best, a work in progress with many shortcomings to be fixed. At worst it is a prison.

2. The Human Conundrum

Before we can talk intelligently about human wildness and domestication, we must first have a clear idea what it means to be human, the extent to which we are a part of nature, and how we interact with it. This is a tall order – one that has been keeping philosophers busy for centuries. In more recent times, it has opened up a whole new field of study called anthropology. It is also a subject rife with socio-political implications, tainted by conflicting cultural values, and underscored by deeply religious presuppositions. To make matters worse, we are not privy to all the facts. No one knows with absolute certainty all there is to know about *Homo sapiens* in particular or about the world at large. So we must tread lightly here.

Formidable obstacles appear a short distance down the long, winding road towards understanding ourselves. The moment we utter the word "human," we enter the morass of morality where people profoundly disagree with each other, where one person's beliefs regarding the matter are fighting words to another. As the British philosopher Mary Midgley put it so well in her book, *Beast and Man*: "All moral doctrines, all practical suggestions about how we ought to live, depend upon some belief about what human nature is like." And there is no consensus. This not to say we shouldn't try to sort this matter out and come to some kind of agreement, but it would be foolish to think there will ever be enough scientific facts, enough empirical evidence, or a convincing enough argument to get everyone on board about what it means to be human. Whatever conclusions the wisest among us reach are sure to draw fire from one corner or another. Such is the human condition.

It is easy to see the wildness and domestication in other animals because, well, because they are not us. Yes, we too are animals, but the fact remains that we are the ones who do the domesticating. The wildness and domestication of other animals is a direct consequence of our control over them, or lack thereof. The same can be said about plants, microbes, and the landscapes we manipulate. The same can be said about our interaction with everything on this planet and beyond. Wildness is, by definition, that which we don't control. By the same token domestication is that which is under our thumb. This much is simple.

What about the domestication of humans? How does that happen? Is it even possible to *completely* domesticate human beings, who are by definition the ones who do the domesticating? Do we domesticate each other? Do we domesticate ourselves? This is a big part of the human conundrum to be sure.

One would think that we would have all this sorted out by now, that with the many advances in science made during the past few hundred years, we would have a clear idea what exactly it means to be human. But, as the early 20th century German philosopher Max Scheler once said: "The special sciences that deal with man, valuable as they are, tend to hide his nature more than they reveal it." In fact, the more we learn about human biology and behavior, the more the matter becomes muddled. Yes, we are animals, but we are something else as well. Yes, we have biological needs like every other animal, but our intense self-awareness creates psychological needs that rise above and beyond our strictly biological ones. Yes, we are self-domesticated creatures, functioning within the context of civilization, but there still remains a streak of wildness in us. In short, we are walking contradictions.

Scheler went on to say, "At no time in his history has man been so much a problem to himself as he is now." That's because we have more information about ourselves now than we've ever had before. We are overwhelmed by it. Meanwhile we live in a global civilization that is so vast, so complex, so all-consuming that it seems to have a life of its own. Collectively, we humans dominate the planet. Individually, we have never been so helpless, with so much of our lives dictated by factors we cannot control. The social contract that we all must abide by – with its many laws, implicit moral values, and various socio-economic relations – forces us to do things we wouldn't otherwise do. Freedom is, for the most part, relegated to the paltry choices we make in the marketplace with our discretionary money, and to how we use what little time we have left after work and other obligations have been met. This situation is maddening, to say the least.

It is maddening because deep down inside we sense that there has to be a better way to live – a healthier, happier way.

Are we completely wild and free creatures? Obviously not, but a part of us wants to be. A part of us wants to return to the Garden of Eden, to a time before all this complexity and workaday nonsense began. Yet we enjoy the conveniences of modern living, don't we? So we are conflicted. We are caged animals quite comfortable in our cages, yet dreaming of breaking away. We are safe and secure in this highly sophisticated society, yet feeling somewhat stifled by it. In short, we are absurd creatures.

There is no going back to the Garden, no reset button. There is only a continuous movement forward from wherever we are now to wherever we are going to be. More importantly, there is no escaping the absurdity of the human condition – the tension between our wild and domesticated selves, the tension between the individual and society at large, and the strain of an all-too-conscious mind considering the infinite possibilities of the universe while being trapped in a finite body. As the existentialist thinker Albert Camus said: "A man who has become conscious of the absurd is forever bound to it." We humans are absurd. Nothing anyone says or does can make this absurdity go away. We either ignore it or deal with it head on. That is all.

The fundamental problem with being human is that we don't really know how or why we came to be. Oh sure, creation myths and sacred texts concerning the origin of man abound, but they are all rooted in one particular culture or another so the stories conflict. More importantly, they are impossible to substantiate. Meanwhile scientists tell us that we've descended from the apes, yet no "missing link" has ever been found between our hominid cousins and us. In other words, evolution doesn't adequately explain the emergence of our *humanity* from an animal past. Not really. "Man is a stream whose source is hidden," Ralph Waldo Emerson wrote a century and a half ago, before Darwin, and it still holds true. Being human is more than making a better tool, venturing into the great unknown, or showing compassion for others. It is all this and something else. And nothing in our past, be it mythical or evidence-based, explains what that something else is… or why human beings exist at all.

Both religious and secular minds alike will scoff at this claim, I'm sure. That's because the morass of morality runs far and wide. Every one of us has an opinion, a belief set, a particular worldview. And most of it is set in stone. Those who embrace reason above all else are the worst offenders, believing as they do that there is a perfectly good explanation for everything and all we have to do is discover it. To them the absurdity of the human condition is rooted in the mumbo-jumbo of religion and other superstitions, and once we get clear of that we'll be home free. Yeah, right. And someday we'll know all there is to know about the universe. Dream on.

I do not advocate surrendering to ignorance, giving up the quest to fully understand ourselves. On the contrary, I believe that self-knowledge is the most important task before us. All other knowledge, as the ancient Greeks liked to say, stems from it. But we should not underestimate the challenge or settle for easy answers when the human condition is anything but easy to comprehend. Tolerance is a key element. A closed mind is good for starting and fighting wars, but lousy at figuring things out. Only the open mind – a mind that seriously considers all possibilities and systematically works its way through them – has a chance of resolving the human conundrum. If we keep our minds open, then perhaps we can reach some general agreement about what we are, what is right and wrong about our interactions with each other, and where we stand in relation to the rest of nature. But that's a tall order, indeed.

3. Wild, Not Wild

Wild, wildness, wilderness. We utter these words as if their meanings are self-evident, and that's how the trouble begins. Like "truth," "love" and "God," the word "wild" is so fraught with implications, with greatly varying ways of seeing the world, that it can signify all sorts of things... and nothing at all. So we must clarify matters before using this word in any serious discussion about human nature or nature as a whole. That means we must consider what is not wild as well as what is wild, and how these concepts relate to the practical realities of the world in which we live.

It is safe to say that the entire world was wild before human beings came along – that wildness and nature were one in the same long ago. It is also safe to say that the emergence of civilizations in the Near East, Asia, the Americas and elsewhere mark a distinct break with the wild world. The domestication of plants, animals and the landscape were well underway by then. Prior to the emergence of civilizations, though, the matter becomes somewhat murky. For tens of thousands of years, when we were hunter/gatherers and more integrated into the natural world than we are today, our impact upon the planet wasn't quite so obvious. But this much is clear: domestication is what separates the wild from the not wild, and that is something we humans do. In fact, we do it to such an extent these days that one has to wonder if anything on our planet remains truly wild at all. What haven't we touched?

Dogs were the first creatures that we domesticated. Their remains have been found in human camps dating back 15,000 years. They have probably been by our sides twice that long. Descended from wolves, they were as much hunters as we were back in the day. They were scavengers to boot. They most likely entered the orbit of human affairs when they started feeding off our garbage piles. Soon thereafter they became our sentinels and hunting companions. That's the theory, anyhow. Truth is, we will never know for certain how or why our ancestors domesticated them. All we do know is that they have been with us for a long, long time.

For the past decade, a long-haired German Shepherd named Matika has been with me on nearly every excursion that I've taken into wild places. I occasionally go for walks in the forest with family and friends without having Matika in tow, but she has been by my side every time I've gone deep into the woods supposedly alone. "Wilderness dog," I like to call her, because she likes tramping through wild forests as much as I do. And she looks quite at home in that setting, sniffing around, skulking about on all fours in her wolfish demeanor. Every once in a while, I have to shout "No!" at her, whenever she finds the remains of some dead animal and starts feasting on it. Her domesticated belly isn't quite equal to the task. All the same, the urge is there. And when a chipmunk or squirrel scurries across the forest floor, she'll dart after it without thinking. So it's clear to me that my canine companion, as domesticated as she may be, still has a wild streak in her.

My dog Matika is not alone in this regard. I have seen other dogs in action and am never surprised by their sudden flashes of wildness. Every once in a while a dog goes feral. Sometimes that dog joins a pack of other feral dogs. Sometimes it joins up with coyotes. Granted, a dog is often just a good meal to a pack of coyotes, but there remains a kinship between canines all the same. There remains a wildness in all dogs that tens of thousands of years of domestication has not completely erased. Despite how we treat them, they remain animals first and foremost. Their domestication is not absolute.

That is why I prefer Matika's company to that of my own kind whenever I venture deep into the woods. She seems to understand how I feel in that setting. And when I stop in the middle of nowhere to make camp, she's just as comfortable there as I am. Despite her domestication and mine, the wild forest is not an alien place. What does this say about her? What does this say about me?

We humans look down upon all other creatures, calling them animals as if that somehow distinguishes them from us. The French philosopher of language Jacques Derrida tells us that, "*Animal* is a word that men have given themselves the right to give." Point well taken.

The words we use are loaded with meaning. Language is linked to our perceptions of self and other. As long as we see ourselves as superior beings, and other creatures as inferior, then wildness and domestication are concepts that apply only to them, not us. In that way we set ourselves up as gods, above the fray, as if we came into existence by divine intervention and have no place in nature. But this simply isn't the case, as any student of prehistory knows. The archeological evidence puts our distant ancestors squarely *in nature*, and the genetic evidence confirms it. We too are animals.

We were animals before we were civilized. We still are. "Biological determinism forces upon human behavior certain invariable sequences," the early 20th century anthropologist Bronislaw Malinowski declared, "which must be incorporated into every culture, however refined or primitive, complex or simple." By this he meant that human beings must eat, sleep, defecate, etc. just like all other animals, despite the ways in which we organize ourselves into societies. We are animals, first and foremost, and wildness is no stranger to us. We are as much a part of nature as any other creature. Even though we humans are the ones who do the domesticating, we remain as wild as our elaborate social structures will allow. That is, we are as wild as we allow ourselves to be.

Ralph Waldo Emerson once mused that the exploration of nature would be a waste of time if it were something foreign and unrelated to us. But that's simply not the case. "No, it is bone of our bone, flesh of our flesh, made of us, as we of it," he concluded. How could it be otherwise? How can we look deeply into nature and not see the reflection of ourselves there?

Wild, not wild. It isn't easy trying to sort it all out. The extent to which human beings once were and still are wild is the issue here, and it's hotly contentious. Many people assume that, as civilized men and women, most of our prehistoric wildness has been bred out of us, and that laws keep the remnants of it in check. They associate wildness with bikers and barbarians, with criminals and vandals, and the sooner those wild urges are vanquished once and for all, the better. That a law-abiding, civilized person could still be wild, well, that's unthinkable. Pressed to its logical conclusion, this implies that only *completely* civilized men and women are fully human, and that wild people are something less than human. This is shaky ground to be sure, enabling some people to believe that they are superior beings – superior to other people who are more like animals. This is the dirty little secret behind every civilization, past and present, and the fundamental justification behind most forms of oppression.

That humans *were* wild once is easy enough to accept, even though some of us do not consider prehistoric or pre-civilized peoples fully human. That humans *are* wild to some extent, well, that's a much harder pill to swallow. Such a concept undercuts the very idea of civilization. After all, *civil-izing* is the process by which we domesticate ourselves. How could we possibly be both wild and domesticated? Are we to assume from this that the process is unfinished, that we are not completely civilized yet? If so, then what exactly would completing this process entail? What would an utterly domesticated human being look like, and would such a creature still be human in any way that we would recognize?

Having spent considerable time in wild places, the contemporary nature writer Paul Gruchow says: "In our most serious moments, our wildness is an unfathomable intellectual puzzle." No doubt he has felt the same wild urges that I have felt and has questioned his own humanity in the process. "Plainly, we are animals," he says, "But just as plainly, we are also something else, something more than, or different from, animals." I concur. As human beings, we are both wild and not wild. We are animals, yes, but we are also highly cognizant, self-aware creatures. To some extent this self-awareness separates us from the rest of nature, but not completely. Our wildness, along with our self-domestication, is an unfathomable puzzle to be sure.

Too much time has passed since we last lived in complete harmony with the natural world. We have forgotten our creature-ness – what it is like to be a part of the earth and the earth only. Even as prehistoric hunter/gatherers, long before the first hints of civilization, we manipulated the natural world, making it better suit our needs. How far back in time would we have to go to find a perfectly natural human being? Would such a person be fully human by any measure we care to use? *Human* wildness is tricky business, indeed.

"Know thyself," the ancient Greek sages liked to say, but what could be more difficult? Each and every one of us looks in the mirror and sees something different. Each of us sees not just a different face or body, but a different interior. Each of us sees a god, an animal, or some other entity. We are human beings, yes, on that we all agree. But there the agreement ends. That's because each of us sees both the world and ourselves in a slightly different way. "No man ever looks at the world with pristine eyes," Ruth Benedict wrote in *Patterns of Culture*, "He sees it edited by a definite set of customs and institutions and ways of thinking." Certainly when it comes to being human, objectivity is impossible. So how are we supposed to know ourselves? What can any of us really know about our wildness, or our essential nature as human beings?

A related problem here is that nature itself is a contentious subject, chock-full of presuppositions and distorted views. Before we can make any sense of human nature, we must first make sense of nature itself. What is it exactly that we are trying to say when we utter the word "nature"? Self-knowledge is critical, no doubt, but nothing can be said about the self without a basic understanding of the world at large. And that's not as easy as it sounds.

4. What Is Nature?

Taken at face value, nature is simply everything that isn't manmade – the vast array of material things that existed before the appearance of human beings, and everything that continues to exist despite our impact. Nature is the sky, the earth, the oceans, lakes and streams. Nature is the sum total of all the powerful forces that manifest themselves by way of storms, volcanoes, earthquakes, and every other so-called act of God. Nature is wildlife – everything that lives on its own terms in this world, hell-bent upon survival. But there any simplistic understanding of nature ends. Nature is all this and more. Much more.

Nature is every physical thing in this world, but it is also the universe at large, with all its stars, galaxies and other cosmic phenomena. Nature is every molecule, every atom, subatomic particle, every spark of energy that has or ever will take place. In short, nature is everything, including us. Our all-too-physical bodies are made up of the same elements commonly found in nature. The chemical composition of supernovas and humans are one in the same. We are not alien beings superimposed into an otherwise natural universe. We are a part of it. This cannot be reasonably denied.

If human beings are a part of nature, then the things we make must be a part of nature, as well. Is anything unnatural then? What is nature if nothing exists beyond it? What exactly are we in relation to it? The 19th century Yankee philosopher Ralph Waldo Emerson must have asked himself these questions during his lifetime. "Who are we, and what is Nature, have one answer in the life that rushes into us," he wrote in *Natural History of Intellect*. And that says everything and nothing about the matter, clearly delineating the parameters of the puzzle without saying exactly what the "one answer" is. Life rushes into us. Life flows through nature. Where it comes from and why, well, God only knows.

There is superficial nature – the physical world and everything observable in it – then there is the ghost in the machine. Emerson referred to this phenomenon as the laws of nature. I call it Nature with a capital "N." Most scientists and other rational thinkers call it the laws of physics and hold them sacrosanct. And so they should. But scientists never explain why such laws exist. More to the point, the laws of physics don't explain how life came to be in an otherwise inanimate universe. We now know that the universe expanded from a single point of spacetime roughly 14.7 billion years ago. Even if life came to our planet from elsewhere, it still had to have its origin *somewhere*. That was, by any estimation, an event that took place billions of years *after* the formation of stars and galaxies in our ever evolving universe. So what caused it?

Nature has mind in it. Proof of this is my own mind, as well as that of every other human being – not to mention the many other creatures that *think* to some greater or lesser extent. As the ecological philosopher Max Oelschlaeger asked: "Do we dare think that we are nature watching nature?" That appears to be the case. Our minds facilitate this watching. Unfortunately, our heightened awareness only makes it that much harder for us to see the big picture. We get caught up in the particulars. We can't see the forest for the trees. The whole of nature eludes us, time and again.

Evolution, yes – that explains how things change over time. The incremental development of mind through the ages is easy enough to grasp, but that doesn't explain why something like mind exists at all. The laws of nature insist upon it, as they insist upon the existence of life forms. But where does mind come from and why? What is it about nature that led to the emergence of such a phenomenon? Or has it always existed?

Nature with a capital "N." That's how I see it. Embedded in the universe is the mind of nature from which all things arise, including the so-called laws. In other words, Nature itself determines what does and does not exist. This is a rather pantheistic worldview to be sure, but I can't see how we can explain the universe otherwise. One can utter the word "God" then assert that God creates all things, but how is that different from saying Nature does? The universe operates according to certain physical laws, and those laws must arise from *something*. The only alternative to this line of reasoning is that the laws of nature are themselves the consequence of random acts that took place at the very beginning of spacetime, and that they only *appear* to be sacrosanct. But that's pretty hard to believe. It seems more likely that one thing causes another, as demonstrated time and time again in our world, and that my mind arises from the mind of something else.

Nature and existence. Origins and spacetime. Causation or an utterly random universe. I engage in all this *meta-physical* talk just to show how difficult it is to say anything about nature as a whole without sinking into metaphysics. Most scientists and other rational thinkers like to keep things real, down to earth, dealing only with empirically verifiable facts. But comprehending the whole of nature isn't that simple. We are confounded the moment we ask ourselves: What is nature? This question takes us to the frontier of knowledge and beyond. And any answer we settle upon must ultimately involve us. That makes it subjective. How do I as a human being fit into the greater scheme of things? What exactly does it mean to be human in this world? Ah, back to that again.

More important than any concept of nature that we may conjure up is our practical relationship to it. After all we are, like all other life forms, hell-bent upon survival. Every life form occupies a certain niche or has some advantage. The one thing we humans are really good at is manipulating the natural world to suit our needs. We aren't alone in this, but no other life form can match us. Beavers, for example, build dams. We also build dams, but our impact doesn't stop there. We channelize rivers, build cities and roads, cut down entire forests, extract minerals from the earth, harness the elements for power, domesticate plants and animals, and make all kinds of things. First came the simplest pounding and cutting tools. Now we have electronic devices – very powerful tools, indeed. Now we can rearrange molecules. Now we can split atoms. Now we send spacecraft to the far reaches of the solar system and beyond. What can't we do? Our power seems limitless. All nature, it seems, is ours to control.

But the control of nature is tricky business. Francis Bacon, the godfather of modern science, said it best: "Now the empire of man over things is founded on the arts and sciences alone, for nature is only to be commanded by obeying her." During the Renaissance, while intoxicated with seemingly limitless human potential, Bacon still recognized the power of nature and its sacrosanct laws. "Commanded by obeying her," he cautioned, and that's the kernel of wisdom in his worldview. All our accomplishments in this world, all our technological advances stem from the successful manipulation of nature. We ignore its laws at our peril. We prosper through adaptation to them, and that adaptation must ultimately culminate in a fundamental understanding of nature itself.

What is nature? It is the world we inhabit. It is everything we touch, see, hear, taste, and smell… and then some. It is the set of physical laws that we must obey. It is everything in the universe, including us. That's the most important thing for us to realize. We do not exist in a vacuum. Our actions have consequences so we should be mindful about how we interact with all other entities. On this planet or any other, our well being is inextricably tied to everything else, to that which enables us to exist in the first place.

5. Flirtations with Wildness

As a boy growing up in Ohio, I felt the urge to wildness long before I knew what it was. I was drawn to tales of exploration and adventure, and dreamt of having my own adventures someday. When I was ten, I wandered alone through fallow fields and woodlots on the edge of town, mapping the route in the process so that I could find my way back home. When I was thirteen, I followed streams wherever they took me, and biked dirt roads to neighboring towns with my buddies. I was every helicopter parent's worst nightmare. Fortunately for me, my parents believed that freedom is instrumental to learning responsibility. So I roamed freely.

In my mid-teens, I spent a week canoeing the lake region of northern Wisconsin with a bunch of other Explorer Scouts. That was my first time in wild country. During that trip, when I saw a bald eagle launch itself from a dead tree nearby, a strange feeling emerged from somewhere deep within. I too wanted to spread my wings and soar freely through the world. But a few more years would pass before I'd be able to do that.

In my late teens, I pushed back against Authority as so many teenagers did in the 60s and 70s – as so many teenagers still do. But I was a little wilder and crazier than most kids back then. Sex, drugs and rock'n'roll were not enough for me. I wanted more, much more. So I organized a trip to Kentucky with a few friends to explore the caves there. I took up rock climbing and rappelling. I went skydiving. Then I stuck out my thumb and started hitchhiking. That's when the fun really began.

My best friend at this time was Jeff Armstrong – a fat kid turned bodybuilder with frizzy black hair, an impish grin, and a wild streak almost as wide as my own. Our friendship was cemented on a relatively warm day in early March when we both grabbed hold of the pulley dangling from a cable that stretched across a quarry. While holding onto that pulley, we ran as fast as we could, leaping off the cliff. We shouted with manic joy as we fell into the icy water far below. Shortly thereafter, Jeff accompanied me on an overnight canoe trip on the Mohican River. During that trip he told me over a crackling campfire that I was the only person he knew who seemed to be comfortable in wild places. I wasn't quite sure what he meant by that but, coming from him, it felt like a compliment.

In 1975, when we were roommates at Ohio University, we hitchhiked together to Florida during spring break, before any real hint of spring in Ohio. That was quite the trip. We tented in snowy woods next to the interstate, and rode through the mountains with hillbillies tossing firecrackers at each other inside the car. While standing in freezing rain along a highway just outside Atlanta, Jeff broke away an icicle dangling from my beard, tearing out a few hairs in the process. Then he laughed. That was his way of letting me know we were in the thick of it.

A little over a year later, I stayed with Jeff for a couple days at his apartment in Columbus, Ohio before hitchhiking out west. He had recently moved there after transferring from OU to a technical college. Originally we had planned on doing a big trip out west together, but Jeff couldn't get the time away from his summer job. So he drove me to the edge of town where we said our goodbyes. He motored off to work while I stuck out my thumb.

It was the summer of '76. I was twenty years old with my whole life ahead of me. I had a scraggly beard again. I had cut off my beard when I was an ROTC cadet but had grown it back after quitting the program. I had an old, beat-up, Boy Scout backpack slung over my shoulder and eighty-eight dollars in my pocket. I'd hitchhiked many times before, but never more than a thousand miles at one shot. I told my parents that I was going to the Pacific Northwest to check out a few colleges for post-graduate study. That was about half true. By then I was deep into philosophy. My thoughts had become as wild as my deeds – perhaps even wilder. I had abandoned all conventional ways of seeing the world, and was up to my eyeballs in existential angst. Yeah, I was on the road with a completely open mind – a dangerous arrangement for sure. My youthful exuberance was matched by an overwhelming desire to find something worth believing, some kernel of truth about which I could wrap a brand new worldview. In other words, I was on a vision quest.

I hitchhiked all the way to Seattle then wandered the docks while eating a fresh loaf of sourdough bread, wondering if I should get on the boat now departing for Alaska or perhaps hop a freighter heading for the Far East. I ended up hitchhiking north into British Columbia instead. After a few days in Vancouver, I returned to the States. Then I got it into my head to spend some time in the North Cascade Mountains.

Halfway up a narrow, winding road with hardly any traffic on it, I was beginning to feel like I was stuck in the middle of nowhere. Just then a grinning fellow in a small blue sedan picked me up. We drove up into the mountains as far as the road could take us, until a wall of snow blocked any further progress. Using the cheap plastic tent that I had with me, this perfect stranger and I camped that night on a patch of snow-free ground just above the tree line. Joshua was his name. He was an avid skier. His passion for the mountains matched my own.

In the morning we climbed up through the snow and onto the shoulder of Mount Baker. The sun broke through the clouds illuminating the mountains all around us as we as stood on that ridge. That's when it happened: a wave of divine ecstasy swept over me. Suddenly I could see the face of God manifest in nature, in the wild forest sprawling away from me in all directions. Suddenly it dawned on me that the world is a wild and beautiful place – too magnificent for words. Then Joshua started sliding down the mountain on his street shoes. I followed suit.

I had arrived. I was onto something. My wild urges had brought me to this moment of truth, but what was I to make of it? How was I to translate this ecstatic feeling into a way of life, a worldview? Regarding that, I remained utterly clueless. And the road home was a long, hard one. I stepped on a nail in an abandoned gold mine a few days later, when Joshua and I were touring the Canadian Rockies. That meant I could no longer help him drive his standard shift car. So we parted ways. I limped home, becoming disoriented at one point while crossing the Great Plains. I ran out of money. Yeah, adventure is not always fun.

Back at Ohio University, I finished out my formal study of philosophy, walking away from that hallowed institution of higher learning with a degree in nothingness. By that time my thoughts were wilder than they had ever been. It was an intellectual wildness fueled by all the books I had read, both fiction and nonfiction, and aggravated by the essays, poems and stories I dared to pen. If someone had asked me back then what I believed in, I would have been hard pressed to give a straight answer. I still clung to the Judeo-Christian beliefs of my youth, repackaged as religious existentialism, but in time all that would fade away. Wildness had taken root. Even though another decade or so would pass before that wildness would morph into a worldview, the transformation was underway.

In the summer of '77 I purchased a one-way ticket to Seattle, Washington. Then I boarded a jet with two small bags and a portable typewriter in hand. I set up camp in a rooming house near the University of Washington, took a job working in the college bookstore, and commenced a somewhat dubious career as a fiction writer. Having purchased a beat-up old car, I made a few trips into the Cascade Mountains but did not experience anything even close to what I had experienced on Mt. Baker the year before. No matter. I was back in Ohio before the end of the year, thanks to a rather complicated relationship with a pretty, red-haired young woman named Marge.

Another wild urge sent me to Maine the following summer, but Marge and I moved to Boston and lived together in a basement apartment shortly after that. In Boston I cultivated a rather bohemian, artistic wildness in the company of other writers and poets while Marge worked as a nurse in the nearby hospital. Eventually I talked her into moving out west with me. We landed in Eugene, Oregon in the spring of 1980. I don't think a full month passed before we drove up into the Cascade Mountains for a day. While Marge waited in the car, I speed-hiked two miles to Linton Lake where I spotted a bald eagle in a nest high above the water. Its primal scream echoed through the mountains, shaking me to the core. That's all it took. A couple months later, I was backpacking alone into the Three Sisters Wilderness for five days.

At first I was just another happy hiker tramping along the Pacific Crest Trail, but after lunch on the second day I left the trail, bushwhacking down into Linton Meadows. Soon I was grooving with the wild much the same way I had on the shoulder of Mount Baker, only this time alone and for hours on end. Then I made camp next to the meadows and hung out there for a couple days. I stumbled into a mountain lion while I was in that wilderness. That rocked my world. That's when I realized just how deep into the backcountry I had ventured, and how dangerous a place it could be. But encountering a mountain lion only made me want to spend more time in wild places. Wildness was an itch I had just scratched.

As time went by, I longed for another encounter with a mountain lion. I learned all I could about them while poring through books at the local library. I kept going into the mountains on day hikes, hoping to see one again. This went on for a year. Eventually I stumbled upon the huge, unmistakable tracks of one. I followed them until I reached a ledge overlooking a spot on the switchback trail where I had been less than twenty minutes before. On that ledge was a pile of fresh scat. At first I was intimidated by this, realizing that the lion had just watched me pass below. Then I smiled. Reluctantly, with very little daylight remaining, I left the forest.

Later on that summer, my buddy Jeff came to visit me in Eugene. He was in the Navy by then. The nuclear submarine he was stationed on was temporarily berthed in Portland. He rented a car and suddenly appeared at my doorstep. We talked and laughed and caught up on each other's news. I told Jeff all about my encounter with a mountain lion the year before and the huge tracks I had recently found in the mountains. Would he like to chase down a mountain lion with me? Without hesitation he said: "Yes!" So the next day we drove into the mountains together.

It was just like old times. Jeff and I were having another adventure together. We hiked deep into the forest until I spotted what looked like a fresh set of mountain lion tracks. My pulse raced. I picked up my pace, going farther down the trail. Just then something came over Jeff. He started acting strange, out of character. He said we should start thinking about going back. In my excitement I ignored him, but when he mentioned it a second time I noticed a distinct heaviness in his voice. I stopped, turned around, and looked at him. There was an expression on his face that I had never seen before, as if he was about to break some terrible news to me.

"I have to get back to the boat," he said a third time, "It's getting late." And for a moment we just stood there staring at each other, all too aware of the chasm widening between us.

"Of course," I said, as if I hadn't forgotten about his obligations in my frenzied pursuit of the wild. Then we turned around.

We left the woods, getting back to Eugene that evening. Jeff drove to Portland and reported for duty before he was missed. In the years that followed, we kept in touch, but things were never quite the same between us after that. Two different lives, two entirely different trajectories. All the same, I caught a flash of wildness in Jeff's eyes the last time I saw him, thirty-three years later, right before he died from Parkinson's disease. That part of him never completely went away.

6. Defining the Human

What am I? I call myself a human being, but what exactly does that mean? Preconceived notions get in the way of me understanding what I am. I look in the mirror and see a somewhat hairy, bipedal creature with a prominent forehead and all the biological functions of any other creature. I also see what I have been conditioned to see since I was a child: a being superior to all other creatures, cognitively powerful and self-aware, capable of manipulating the world as no other creature can. In other words, I am *human* therefore something of a god as well as an animal.

This self-image would be ridiculous if it wasn't somewhat true. My kind has dominated this planet for quite some time now. Oh sure, when taken by surprise by a top-of-the-food-chain predator like a crocodile, shark, or tiger, a human being can be eaten, but there isn't a creature alive that we can't capture and put in a cage. Oh sure, when Mother Nature flexes her muscle – a big wind, a natural disaster, or a disease – we take a beating. But here we are, eight billion strong and counting. And we are virtually everywhere, from the arctic to the equator, from the highest mountain to the deep sea. Okay, maybe we haven't gotten down into all the deepest oceanic trenches yet, but give us time. We'll get there eventually. What's to stop us? After all, we've been to the moon and back.

I speak for my entire species when I make these claims, of course. What *we* can do is quite different from what *I* or any other person can do. My individual intelligence is no match for the collective intelligence of humankind. More to the point, *I* can be eaten, *I* can fall victim to a natural disaster, and *I* can die from disease. In fact, I will die from something. That's for certain. Yet I am one of the gods. That's how the matter is muddled, anyhow. I confuse my humanity with collective humanity, leading me to believe that because *we* are gods, *I* am one. But a little time alone in a big enough pocket of wild country convinces me otherwise. In wild country, I confront the hard truth of my physical limitations. Alone in wild country, I am humbled back to my animal self.

So what am I? If I am not a god, then what am I? More than just another animal, certainly. Yes, I have biological functions like every other creature, but there is more to me than that. I think, speak and act as no other creature can. So what exactly am I and how did I get this way?

Defining the human is no easy task. The moment we try to understand our humanity, we slip into the morass of morality where opinions greatly differ. As human beings, we are capable to doing so much, but not everything we do is for the best. Both good and evil factor into our humanity. How we define good and evil says a great deal about how we define ourselves... and vice versa. The trouble began long ago, with the first utterances of religion and philosophy coming out of our mouths, and continues to this day. That much we can all agree upon. But which thoughts and actions of ours are good and which of them are evil? That is where we disagree. More to the point, when we try to define the human, a fundamental question arises: Is a human being in its natural state basically good or basically evil? Ah, I can feel myself sinking into morass right now, can't you?

The 17th century English philosopher Thomas Hobbes is commonly associated with the man-is-basically-evil worldview. He put forth a strong argument in favor of central authority, which he believed is a prerequisite to any civilization worthy of the name. In his book *Leviathan*, he considered the natural condition of humankind to be a war "of every man against every man." Without a central authority – what he called "a common power" – human beings are like dogs fighting over bones. It is central authority, and all the trappings of a stratified society that go with it, that keeps us in check. In a purely natural state, Hobbes said, the life of man is "solitary, poor, nasty, brutish and short." The presumption here is that before civilization human beings behaved worse than animals and were utterly miserable as a consequence. Hobbes paints a grim picture of human nature, indeed.

A century later the French philosopher Jean Jacques Rousseau saw things differently, vehemently disagreeing with Hobbes. In his *Discourse on Inequality*, he wrote: "Compassion is a natural feeling, which, by moderating the violence of love of self in each individual, contributes to the preservation of the whole species." Consequently, Rousseau is associated with the man-is-basically-good worldview. To overcome the evils of self-interest, *the people* create a social contract based upon their general will. Collective action, according to this esteemed French philosopher, is civilization at its best. "The general will is always right and always tends to the public utility," Rousseau asserted in his book, *Of the Social Contract*. He goes on to say: "The people are never corrupted but are often deceived and only then appear to will what is bad." Wow! What great creatures we are collectively!

Hobbes sounds about right to the conservative ear. Liberals prefer Rousseau. But is either one of these worldviews an accurate account of human nature? What facts do Hobbes and Rousseau present to support their claims? What facts do they both overlook? Does either one of them get us out of the morass?

"Man is a part of the universe," the naturalist John Burroughs wrote towards the end of his life, "All that we call good in him, and all that we call bad, are a part of the universe." This is not news. Of course we are a part of the universe. What else could we be? Of course all the good and evil that we do is a part of the universe, because we exist in this universe not elsewhere. Burroughs didn't say anything about human nature that isn't obvious to everyone. Yet the implication here undercuts the more simplistic worldviews of the esteemed philosophers Hobbes and Rousseau. If we as human beings are as bad as Hobbes thinks we are when left to their own devices, yet as good as Rousseau suggests we can be, then we are capable of doing just about anything.

Genghis Khan and Gandhi. Hitler and Martin Luther King. Vlad the Impaler and Mother Theresa. They were all human beings. We want to believe that absolute good and absolute evil are supernatural forces, yet history proves otherwise. We human beings – you, me, and everyone else – are capable of anything and everything. Can we live with this? How much easier it is to embrace a strictly positive or negative view of human nature. How much easier to see our souls as glasses that are either half empty or half full, thereby avoiding the paradox of being both.

If we do not embrace either Hobbes or Rousseau, then how are we to define human nature? Recently I stumbled upon a possible solution in a most unlikely place – a dated work of sociobiology called *Promethean Fire*. Its authors Charles J. Lumsden and Edward O. Wilson wrote: "The theory of human nature that prevails in the end will be one that aligns social behavior and history with all that is known about human biology." When first reading this statement, I marveled at its elegance. I am still impressed by it. The gist of it is quite simple really – simple yet not simplistic. When finally we have the courage to look at the *complete* historical record and match that against everything science can tell us about ourselves, we will be able to put together a fairly clear picture of what we are, thus escaping the morass.

We live on a planet. We inhabit its biosphere. We are a part of the global ecosystem. We interact with each other and all other natural phenomena on this planet. We have done so for thousands upon thousands of years. The truth about what we are rests in our historical documents, our archeological findings, the fossil record, and the human genome combined. How are we to define human nature, *our* nature? Simply by looking at the facts.

The longstanding quest to understand ourselves and therefore define the human reached a critical juncture in 1859 with the publication of Charles Darwin's *On the Origin of Species*. In that book Darwin outlined the principle of evolution by natural selection. A decade later he published *The Descent of Man*, in which he applied the principle of natural selection to humankind. "Those naturalists who admit the principle of evolution," he declared in that book, "Will feel no doubt that all the races of man are descended from a single primitive stock." In other words, humankind evolved into its current state of being from some kind of primordial, ape-like creature. The bones examined in Darwin's day suggested as much. The similarity between human bones and those of the great apes were too compelling to be ignored, and some of the oldest bones dug up seemed to be a mix of the two. A hundred and fifty years later, those of us who take the principle of evolution the least bit seriously accept the "descent of man" as a fact. Does this get us out of the morass of morality? Not entirely, but it's a place to start.

How then are we to devise a reasonable definition of the human? Begin at the beginning. We must go back to our origins deep in nature and trace our development from the creatures we once were to the ones we are today. To theorize about human nature before doing so is pointless. We are what we have become over great periods of time. If we pay careful attention to what we discover in our past, not flinching at those aspects of our nature that we find distasteful, we just might arrive at the truth about ourselves. If not, we will flail about in the morass of morality indefinitely.

7. Hominids

We are creatures inhabiting a planet that orbits a star in an outer arm of the Milky Way Galaxy, which is one of billions of galaxies in the universe. Despite the loftiest notions we may entertain about ourselves, this simple fact remains. It would be foolish to ignore this fact while trying to understand what we are exactly. First and foremost, we are physical creatures living in a physical universe.

The 19th century English biologist Thomas H. Huxley did not ignore this fact. In his book *Evidence as to Man's Place in Nature*, he wrote: "The question of questions for mankind – the problem which underlies all others, and is more deeply interesting than any other – is the ascertainment of the place which Man occupies in nature and of his relations to the universe of things." Other biologists of his day felt the same way, so they started looking at the bones of human beings and how they compare to the bones of various animals. Curiously enough, they found that human skeletons bear a striking similarity to those of the great apes – namely orangutans, gorillas and chimpanzees. Then a few very old bones were excavated that taxonomists had a difficult time classifying as either human or animal.

In 1871 Charles Darwin published his book, *The Descent of Man,* in which he directly addressed the matter of human evolution. He pulled no punches. He went after the superiority of the human mind, which is the one thing that clearly separates us from the rest of creation. "The difference in mind between man and the higher animals, great at it is, is certainly one of degree and not of kind," he wrote, sparking a controversy that continues to this day. Creationists take a different view, of course, declaring that man was made in God's image and therefore stands apart from the animals. Evolutionists remind us that all the paleontological findings to date support Darwin's claim. More importantly, recent analysis of the human genome supports it. Not only are we genetically similar to the great apes, roughly 98 percent of our genes are the same as our closest non-human relative, the chimpanzee.

Due to the mounting evidence, scientists now place human beings squarely in the family *Hominidae.* In other words, we are classified as hominids, or great apes, along with gorillas, orangutans and chimpanzees. From an evolutionarily standpoint, we split first with orangutans and gorillas. Then, roughly 4 to 8 million years ago, we finally broke with chimpanzees.

As our closest, non-human relative, chimpanzees can teach us a lot about ourselves. For decades Jane Goodall studied chimps in their natural habitat in Tanzania, Africa, meticulously recording their interactions with each other. "There is a great deal in chimpanzee social relations to remind us of our own behavior," she concluded, "More, perhaps, than many of us would care to admit." Chimpanzees commonly demonstrate both compassion and coldness towards each other. They laugh, show anger, cry, practice deception, demonstrate empathy, develop interpersonal bonds, hug each other, attack and occasionally kill each other. They use sticks as levers, stones to break open nuts, and blades of grass to extract termites from mounds. All this draws into question the differences between human beings and animals. Perhaps Darwin was right. Perhaps the differences between us and the other animals are more "one of degree and not of kind." All the same, it seems rather heretical to even consider that possibility. Are we not gods compared to the other animals? Just look at what we've accomplished!

Our break with the chimps was well underway 4 million years ago with the emergence of *Australopithecus* – a large-brained, bipedal hominid. The Australian anthropologist Raymond Dart discovered the bones of the first *Australopithecus* in South Africa in 1924. Several other variations of *Australopithecus* have been found since then, each with slightly different qualities, but all quite distinct from the chimpanzee genus, *Pan*. Bipedalism is the dead giveaway. Chimps can walk upright for short distances, but their skeletons are not really designed for extended travel that way. *Australopithecus*, on the other hand, was built similar to us. All variations of *Australopithecus* have been extinct for quite some time now – for millions of years. Still it is commonly believed that our own genus, *Homo*, arose from this stock.

As Richard Leakey says in his book, *The Origin of Humankind*: "Human prehistory evidently took a major turn 2 million years ago." That is when *Homo erectus* arrived on the scene – a creature with many of the characteristics that we commonly associate with being human. *Homo erectus* was the first human-like creature to fashion stone tools and use them on a regular basis. *Homo erectus* was also the first hominid to harness fire. As the name suggests, these creatures walked fully erect. They could actually run on their two legs. That gave them a big advantage over all other hominids. Their bodies were considerably larger than *Australopithecus*, as were their brains. That means they needed a lot more calories so meat eating became their primary means of subsistence. They lived in bands not unlike modern hunter/gatherers, and probably had some loose social organization that we moderns would find similar to our own. Although originally African, they ranged throughout Eurasia. These were not creatures limited to any particular ecosystem. They were all about adaptation.

Evolution is messy business. The *Homo* lineage isn't as clear-cut as we'd like to think it is. Our family tree has a lot of detours and dead-ends in it. *Homo habilis* and *Homo rudolfensis* were ape-men that predate *Homo erectus* and blur the line between the various *Australopithecus* and *Homo* species. *Homo ergaster* is now considered an early version of *Homo erectus*. Fast forward to half a million years ago and *Homo heidelbergensis* arrives on the scene – the predecessor to our own species, *Homo sapiens*. To complicate matters even further, *Homo floresiensis* –

supposedly a variety of *Homo erectus* – lived as recently as a hundred thousand years ago, when the earliest versions of our species, *Homo sapiens*, were roaming the earth. Messy business, indeed, adding further credence to Darwin's claim that the difference between us and every other human-like creature that has ever existed is more "one of degree and not of kind." Disturbing to say the least. Disturbing because the harder we look into the deep past, trying to determine what it is exactly that makes us human, the less clear it becomes where nature ends and our humanity begins.

Since the late 18th century, true believers in The Great Chain of Being have searched long and hard for the "missing link" – for that particular human-like creature that bridges the gap between the human and animal worlds. The Great Chain of Being is a concept dating back to the 3rd century Neoplatonic philosopher, Plotinus. It holds that all being is hierarchal, moving from the most primitive forms towards ultimate perfection. This concept went out of vogue in intellectual circles during the late 19th century, but Arthur O. Lovejoy breathed new life into it in 1936 with the publication of his book: *The Great Chain of Being: the Study of the History of an Idea*. To a greater or lesser extent, most religions assume this hierarchy, as do most humanist worldviews. That is why the vast majority of people see humankind as the pinnacle of nature. Are not our many achievements proof of it? So the question remains: what creature is the "missing link" out of which our humanity emerged?

    The more we look into human evolution, the

more our humanity becomes muddled. It becomes muddled despite the fact that some of us are hell-bent upon finding the "missing link,' thus proving our natural superiority over the rest of the animal kingdom. As hard as we may look, no such "missing link" ever emerges. In human prehistory, all we ever find are incremental changes.

I am inclined to believe what Alan Walker and Pat Shipmen wrote in their book, *The Wisdom of the Bones*: "The 'missing link' is an artificial construct and an unholy grail." We start with a false assumption about our superiority then try to prove it. There is no "missing link" because the hierarchy that we perceive in nature (with ourselves at the pinnacle) does not really exist. There is only nature in its infinite varieties, and us squarely in the thick of it.

So what about all these brainy hominids? How do they fit into the greater scheme of things? Why did they come into being? More to the point, what is the genus *Homo* all about? Since we are the last surviving species of this genus, it is ourselves that we are talking about here, of course. It seems our very existence in this world, as *thinking* creatures, is a great mystery. To unravel this mystery, it helps to have some idea what we are exactly. To understand what we are, it helps to have some idea where we came from – when and how our particular species, *Homo sapiens*, came into being.

One thing is clear: becoming human had a lot to do with the mechanisms of hunting and gathering. Our distant ancestors were hunter/gatherers for over a million years – long before any semblance of civilization, or the systematic domestication of plants that accompanied it. As the American professor of mythology Joseph Campbell observed: "This physical body of ours, of which our psyche is a function, evolved under the conditions not of agriculture but of the hunt." *Homo erectus* was a hunter/gatherer, as all *Homo sapiens* were until ten or fifteen thousand years ago. In fact, there are a few humans living today who are still hunter/gatherers. Not only was the hunt a big part of our past, but that part of us has not yet completely disappeared.

What else do we know about our deep past? Along with being hunter/gatherers, our distant ancestors were migrators. Unlike other hominids that stay pretty close to the equator, our kind has spread across the entire globe. *Homo sapiens* can now be found everywhere from the equator to the poles, on every continent and most islands. We are creatures on the move. This migration began *before* we were fully human – back in the early days of *Homo erectus*. Other waves of *Homo* followed until finally our particular species emerged out of Africa. As the anthropologist F. Clark Howell wrote back in the 1990s: "There is now a consensus that the *ultimate* roots of *Homo sapiens* are African." The genetic information that has been compiled during the past few decades confirms this.

In 1987 Rebecca Cann and her colleagues published a paper in the journal *Nature* giving considerable credence to this "Out of Africa" theory. She had collected samples of mitochondrial DNA (mtDNA) from women all over the globe, revealing the migrations and mutations of peoples over time, and showing that all *Homo sapiens* can be traced back to the first woman, or group of women, living in south/central

Africa somewhere between 100,000 and 200,000 years ago. This mother of our species is commonly referred to as the Mitochondrial Eve. As Cann put it in another paper written a few years later: "Work on mtDNA in modern humans suggests that there was widescale replacement of many archaic people by African lineages with limited gene flow." In other words a single species, *Homo sapiens*, migrated out of Africa and into the rest of the world, effectively pushing every other species of *Homo* out of existence.

We moderns, being so accustomed to conflict, are inclined to think in terms of conquest – that our species pushed out every other human-like species by sheer force. But it's more likely that our distant ancestors were simply better hunters than those they encountered. Food is, after all, the key to survival. *Homo sapiens* developed throwing spears. That's a big advantage over thrusting ones, which is what every other species of *Homo* used. After all, killing an animal from a distance is much easier than trying to sneak up and stab it.

What does all this talk about the distant past tell us about ourselves? First and foremost, it shows that we have emerged from nature – that a human being is as much a creature of the earth as any other creature. Humans came into being gradually, over millions of years, from early primates to man-apes walking erect, to human-like creatures, and ultimately to the people we are today. It tells us that we have been hunter/gatherers for a long, long time. It also tells us that being bipedal creatures with big brains has worked to our great advantage, enabling us to migrate into and adapt to a wide variety of climates and habitats. We are toolmakers, and that too has been instrumental to our success.

We are hominids. That much is certain. Still something is missing from this story. What ultimately makes us human? We have searched for that "missing link," between the rest of nature and ourselves, and have found nothing. Darwin tells us that the differences between us and all other animals is "one of degree and not of kind," but that is not helpful. Not really. A chimp, as genetically close to us as they are, is not human. Somewhere along the line, we *became* human. That is, we *evolved* into our humanity. So what is it? What is the one thing about us that truly separates us from the rest of nature?

"The animality of man we can grasp with a fair degree of clarity," the theologian Abraham J. Heschel said, "The perplexity begins when we attempt to make clear what is meant by the *humanity* of man." Indeed. Our fundamental humanity is the issue here. Science has brought our animality to light, thus establishing a direct connection between nature and us, and therefore between wildness and being human. Yet something in the scientific description of *Homo sapiens* is missing. Science has not established what it is exactly that makes us human, fully human.

Nowadays anthropologists differentiate between *anatomically* modern humans and *behaviorally* modern humans. That is, they see a difference between those who simply look like us and those who think and act as we do. Ms. Cann and her colleagues gave us a fairly good idea what constitutes an anatomically modern human. In that regard, Mitochondrial Eve is the missing link between our species and all others. But a behaviorally modern human is something else altogether. To better grasp the transformation into behaviorally modern humans, we must turn to the physical evidence left behind by our not-quite-so-distant ancestors. What makes us fully human? The answer, it seems, is painted on rocks and the walls of caves.

8. The Emergence of Fully Human Beings

The difference between an *anatomically* modern human and a *behaviorally* modern human is huge. It's easy enough to look like a human being; quite another to think and act like one. The change in behavior is evident in the stone tools and other artifacts left behind by our direct ancestors. A major cultural transformation took place during the Upper Paleolithic, somewhere between 60,000 and 40,000 years ago, and we were the end result – fully human beings.

As the evolutionary biologist John T. Bonner reminds us, culture is not limited to humans. Animals have cultures as well. "By culture I mean the transfer of information by behavioral means, most particularly by the process of teaching and learning." What we call instinct is hardwired into the genes of animals, but how does that information get there in the first place? That's where learning comes into play, and it is as old as animals themselves. But long after our species, *Homo sapiens,* first came into being, we started learning incredibly fast, and in surprisingly new ways that distinguished us from all other creatures.

For well over a hundred thousand years, *Homo sapiens* shared this planet with another species of *Homo*, the Neanderthals. Neanderthals are our closest human-like relatives – so close that some say they were human and should be classified as such: *Homo sapiens neanderthalis* to our *Homo sapiens sapiens*. They are so close to us that distinctly Neanderthal traits exist in the human genome. That means we must have interbred with them at some point. But Neanderthals were significantly different from us. For one thing, they weren't very sophisticated in their tool-making, living arrangements or hunting techniques. Neither were our direct ancestors – the first *Homo sapiens* who lived 100,000 years ago. But something happened to our direct ancestors about the time they migrated out of Africa that didn't happen to Neanderthals.

The big change took place in our brains. As the British anthropologist Christopher Stringer stated in an article recently published in the journal *Nature*: "Some of the known differences in coding DNA between Neanderthals and recent humans are associated with brain development and function." Not just a change in the *quantity* of brain mass – something that had been going on for millions of years – but in the *quality* of it. In other words, what makes us fully human is hardwired into our brains, into our cerebral cortex to be specific.

The paleoanthropologist Richard Klein made an interesting comment in his book, *The Dawn of Human Culture*: "Virtually everyone agrees that before 60,000 years ago, the Neanderthals were alone in Europe and after 30,000 years ago they were gone." What happened to them? At that time *behaviorally* modern humans, a variety of *Homo Sapiens* called Cro-Magnons, migrated into their continent. For one thing, Cro-Magnons had throwing spears while Neanderthals had only thrusting ones. That's a big advantage when it comes to hunting. The Neanderthals tried to duplicate these and other Cro-Magnon tools but with little success. Something just didn't click in the Neanderthal brain. So the Neanderthals perished, along with the Denisovans in Asia and all other humanlike species scattered across the planet at that time. They simply couldn't compete. As Christopher Stringer put it, "The Neanderthals probably went out with a whimper, not a bang."

So what was the big change that took place in the Cro-Magnon brain? It is difficult to say for certain because the brain doesn't survive the press of time the way bones do. But we can draw some strong inferences from the artifacts left behind by Cro-Magnons. The standardization of tools, body decorations, figurines, storage facilities, structured hearths, the organization of living spaces, and ritualized burials – all this is what the archaeologist and anthropologist Ofer Bar-Yosef sees "as evidence for rapid technological changes, emergence of self-awareness and group identity." More importantly, he sees in Cro-Magnon artifacts "the ability to symbolically record information." Anything suggesting that is evidence of a sophisticated language.

"The last key neural change promoted the modern capacity for rapidly spoken phonemic language," Klein says, stating what he believes is the best explanation for the dawn of human culture. This follows not only from the artifacts left behind by our distant ancestors, but also from what we now know about the power of language itself. "Language is a force for change, for exchanging ideas, and for complex thought," the popular writer Brian Fagan declared in his book *Cro-Magnon*. This statement certainly sheds light on that critical moment in human development when we combine it with what the cognitive psychologist Stephen Pinker points out: "Simple logic says there can be no learning without innate mechanisms to do the learning." Well now... does anything facilitate learning and the communication of ideas as well as language?

The key to understanding what makes us fully human is painted on rocks and across cave walls in southern Europe and elsewhere. Prehistoric rock art has been found all over the planet – from Africa to Indonesia and Australia, throughout Eurasia, and into the Americas. Some of this art dates back 40,000 years or more – back to when *behaviorally* modern humans were just coming into their own. Painted figures, mostly of hunted animals, are common throughout the world, along with various abstract shapes and assorted symbols. This is not the handiwork of subhuman creatures. These prehistoric artists were as cognizant as we are – communicative, capable of complex thought, and self-aware.

    In 1868, the paleontologist Louis Lartet excavated prehistoric human remains along with the bones of extinct animals at a Cro-Magnon rock shelter near the village of Les Eyzies. These Cro-Magnon bones were morphologically distinct from the Neanderthal ones that had been found in Germany a dozen years earlier, but nearly as old. In 1879, cave paintings were found in the Altamira cave located in southern Spain – the handiwork of Cro-Magnons. In the decades that followed, more Cro-Magnon art was found in 300 other caves scattered throughout southern France and Spain. The Chauvet Cave, discovered in the 1990s, contains some of the most remarkable cave art with figurative paintings dating back well over 30,000 years. This suggests that fully human beings have been around a long time – much longer than the cities and civilizations that we commonly associate with our humanity.

"Many species communicate, but only humans have language, and only humans communicate through symbols," the anthropologist Alan Barnard wrote in his book *Genesis of Symbolic Thought*. "To use symbolism is to be human," he goes on to say. Abstract thought takes place in the cerebral cortex – in the frontal lobe to be specific. Look around you. Your fellow human beings all have that prominent forehead where the frontal lobe sits. So did Cro-Magnons. Now look at photos of the skulls of Homo erectus, or even our closest cousins, the Neanderthals. The prominent forehead is just not there.

No doubt all other species of *Homo* were capable of thinking to some extent, as all hominids are. All mammals think. My dog certainly thinks. I've seen her in action. One could argue that all creatures think, if learning is an indication of some kind of basic thought process going on. That much said, human beings are capable of thinking on an entirely different plane. Like all other creatures, we think concretely about whatever information our senses provide. But we can also think abstractly, in ways that are not directly related to the immediate environment or our perception of it. Abstraction is where symbols come from. "Symbolization is the essential act of mind," the philosopher Suzanne K. Langer declared, "and mind takes in more than what is commonly called thought."

We symbolize therefore we are human. That much is clear. But how did it happen? How did we get this way? The sociologists Emile Durkheim and Marcel Mauss believed that it all began with our awareness of what is us and what is not us. In their book *Primitive Classification*, they wrote: "Humanity in the beginning lacks the most indispensible conditions for the classificatory function." In other words, categorizing things is the symbolic mind at work. But we haven't always had that ability. We grew into it. "The first logical categories were social categories," Durkheim and Mauss went on to say. Father, mother, uncle, son, sister, cousin, etc. – these categories were essential to primitive social organization. They were most likely the first abstract words ever used. There's no way to prove or disprove this theory, of course, but it does bring to light an important fact: organizations of any sort, and social organizations in particular, are inextricably entwined with communication. And human language is by far the most effective way to communicate.

The anthropologist Clifford Geertz believed, as Max Weber did, that "Man is an animal suspended in webs of significance he himself has spun." Geertz sees culture as the sum total of those webs, so any interpretation of culture is essentially one of meaning. Taking this train of thought further, he said that,

"Culture is public because meaning is." I don't know if I completely agree with this conclusion, but I can see how he reached it. The meaning we give our lives is all wrapped up in our understanding of the world, and that understanding is both symbolic and communicative. Through language we bounce ideas off each other, and that's where meaning comes from. According to Geertz, that is where human culture comes from. This would explain all those images and symbols painted on cave walls, anyhow. The artists who drew them definitely had ideas that they wanted to convey to others.

In some ways the artwork painted on rock walls by Cro-Magnons tens of thousands of years ago are still a mystery to us. Because the people who painted those walls are dead and gone, we do not know what exactly their images and symbols are supposed to mean. In this regard, Cro-Magnon culture remains alien. Or is it? After contemplating the 25,000-year old paintings in the Apollo 11 Cave in southern Africa, Alan Barnard took another view. He saw similarities between the shamanic practices depicted in those paintings and the well-documented practices and artwork of the San people who live in the Kalahari Desert today. "There is almost certainly a cultural continuity between the rock art of southern Africa and the present-day hunter-gatherer inhabitants of the Kalahari," Bernard wrote. If that's the case, then what's the fundamental difference between Cro-Magnons and us? Is there one?

At the beginning of the 20th century, a young priest name Henri Breuil took an interest in prehistoric art. He spent considerable time in the Altamira cave and elsewhere studying cave paintings. Breuil is best known for his sketched interpretation of "The Sorcerer" in the Trois Frères Cave. In a recently published book, *The Cave Painters*, Gregory Curtis wrote: "Breuil believed that art began with a desire for disguise, in particular disguise with masks." Supposedly these masks helped Cro-Magnon hunters get closer to their prey. "That, according to Breuil, 'convinced man that the mask or disguise itself possessed a ghostly magical power.'"

Alan Barnard and Henri Breuil aren't the only ones to suggest that prehistoric cave art had something to do with rites and rituals. Such interpretations are common among those who study the origins of religion and human culture. In his landmark work, *The Idea of the Holy*, Rudolf Otto coined the term *mysterium tremendum*, which translates roughly to "the awesome mystery." Therein lies the essence of all spiritual and religious sentiment, and what our Cro-Magnon ancestors must have felt just as deeply as we do. "It is this feeling which, emerging in the mind of primeval man, forms the starting-point for the entire religious development in history," Otto says. And rightly so. Once one becomes both self-aware and cognizant of the world, one senses the yawning chasm between what we know and what we don't know about the world and ourselves. If I had lived 40,000 years ago, I too would have painted on rock walls, doing my best to come to terms with the great unknown. That is, after all, what we philosophers and theologians do.

The awesome mystery. A modern-day skeptic may scoff at this notion, but that doesn't make it any less real to those of us who look skyward on a starry night and ponder the meaning of things and our place in the universe. I can only imagine how the stars must have affected Cro-Magnons back in their day. Regardless how they interpreted the world around them, and how those interpretations differ from ours, cave art makes it clear that Cro-Magnon people were unquestionably human. They were more like those of us living today than we are willing to admit.

9. I, Cro-Magnon

For a while I made a half-hearted attempt to suppress my wildness and live a somewhat normal life. After living in Oregon for a year and a half, my live-in girlfriend Marge was homesick and unhappy, so we packed up the car and drove back east. We headed for Chicago in order to be closer to her family in Ohio. With the hope of creating some kind of emotional stability for ourselves, we got married along the way. We lived in Chicago just long enough for me to make plans for us to start a small business somewhere in the northeast. And that's what we did. In the summer of '82, we landed in Burlington, Vermont and opened a used bookstore. I was proud of myself for doing something responsible, respectable and mature for a change. But Marge was still unhappy. Vermont didn't work for her. She wanted to live in Ohio, not some place a day's drive away from it. Unfortunately, I didn't feel that way, so our rather tenuous marriage came apart at the seams. The following year, I helped Marge move back to Ohio. Then I returned to Vermont to mind the store. A month later, I filed for divorce.

Wildness was an itch I had scratched in the

Oregon backcountry. I wanted more of that. No sooner was the divorce finalized and I was making plans to sell the store and buy a one-way ticket to Alaska – the wildest place that I could reach without leaving the United States. I would use the proceeds from the sale of the store to provision myself. Then I would disappear into the Alaskan bush and live off the land. Yeah, I started reading, researching and making plans to that effect. But the more I looked into it, the more I realized that disappearing into the bush is pretty much the same as dying there. Lots of wild-eyed young men like me had already done just that. So I scrapped the plan and kept minding the store until I could figure out a better way to cultivate my wildness.

Judy Ashley entered my life in the spring of '85. By then I had grown accustomed to being single, the bookstore was humming along nicely, and I was in a good enough place emotionally to have a relationship with an intelligent, attractive, self-assured woman like her. We hit it off from the start. But while our relationship flowered, I took more and more short trips into the nearby Green Mountains, still scratching the itch of wildness. In due time Judy and I got married. Then I sold the store and started working as a guide for a company called Vermont Hiking Holidays. For several years I took small groups of urbanites into the woods on day hikes. That scratched my wild itch even more. Then one day Judy and I had a soulful, no-holds-barred discussion. She asked me what I wanted more than anything else. I surprised myself by saying that I still wanted to go to Alaska – not to live there but to experience bona fide wilderness just once in my life. "Then you should do it," Judy said. So I started making plans to do just that.

Alaska! I could hardly believe what was happening when the jet touched town in Juneau in the summer of '92. I was really doing this. After I spent a day in Juneau collecting supplies that couldn't be carried onto the jet, a bush pilot strapped me into the back seat of a small, single-prop airplane. An hour later, I was standing next to a partially overgrown gravel airstrip with a hundred and twenty-five pounds of food, clothing and equipment piled on the ground next to me, watching that plane fly away. The first thing I did was shove six shells into a .44 magnum revolver – what the Forest Service people told me was minimum protection against bears. Kodiak bears were thick in the Endicott River Wilderness where I had just landed. After orienting myself, I cached a portion of my supplies in the trees next to the airstrip then picked up the rest and headed for the river. It was about two miles away.

The plan was to establish a base camp near the mouth of the Endicott River then backpack upstream, deeper into the wilderness. But I never ventured more than three miles from base camp during my two-week sojourn in the Alaskan bush. On the sweaty slog through the coastal meadow during the first day, I stumbled upon bear paw prints twice as big as my boot, pressed two inches deep into the ground. That changed everything. I panicked at first, immediately slinging all my food bags up into the nearest trees. An hour or so later, once I got over the initial shock of seeing those huge bear paw prints, I took down my food bags, repacked everything, and continued my slog to the river. Upon reaching the river, I made camp. There I went into survival mode, and stayed that way during the rest of the trip.

A few days later, after encountering the biggest bear in the valley, I realized that staying alive and in one piece in the bush would take some doing. Keeping my food away from bears and other pesky critters was the main thing. I slung my food bags fifteen feet into the trees. Fresh water was no problem since it rained every day. I used pans to collect the rainwater running off my tarp. Staying warm and dry during the night wasn't difficult. All I had to do was take off my dry clothes at the beginning of each day and put on damp ones. That way I always had dry clothes to wear when I went to bed. But there were other more insidious threats to my well being. Once I tried to ford the river and almost drowned in the process. My legs grew numb in the icy water. Once I tried to hack my way through the chest-high, thorny devil's club that thickly covered the forest floor. It whacked me in the eye as a result. Soon it dawned on me that being alone in the Alaskan bush was a very dangerous proposition, and that I would have to be smart about what I did. Real smart.

I stayed off the trails because, well, all the trails were bear trails. I yelled "Yo, coming through!" whenever I tramped through the trackless bush so that I wouldn't surprise a sleeping bear. I kept a pile of dry firewood beneath the tarp at all times so that I could start a fire and get warm whenever a chill shot through me. I didn't do anything stupid, or at least tried not to. Slowly, ever so slowly, fear and loneliness gave way to a comfortable wariness and deep solitude. Eventually I felt at home in the vast, sprawling wilderness.

One evening, a week and a half into my Alaskan sojourn, the sky began to clear. I was fixing dinner at the time but had difficulty focusing on the simple task. I kept looking up, amazed by the surrounding landscape. I could hardly believe my eyes. The clouds broke open, exposing a deep blue sky and the Kakuhan Range beneath it. Those magnificent mountains rose abruptly on far side of the broad waterway stretched before me – a fiord called the Lynn Canal into which the Endicott River emptied. Glaciers nestled in the recesses between the jagged, snow-capped peaks of that range, as they did in the Chilkat Range behind me. The landscape all around me looked raw, incredibly wild and primordial. It was as if the Ice Age had just ended.

Here I was immersed in a new world – a world so harsh yet beautiful that it defied description. I gazed upon the half-frozen world around me the same way my distant ancestors must have gazed upon it 15,000 years earlier. That's all the time that had elapsed between the heyday of Cro-Magnons and my own arrival here. No more. What's the difference between them and me? They wore skins; I wear cotton, synthetics and wools. Their tools were of stone and bone; mine are steel and plastic. As the sun waned that evening, I fed sticks into a campfire the same way they once did. I danced and sang around the campfire, as they once did. I thanked god for being alive and well, just as they must have in their day.

As the flames leapt before me, I stood in the middle of that harsh yet beautiful landscape feeling the utter joy of simply living on a planet so perfectly suited to my needs. This is my habitat – this wild, green, watery world stretching for thousands of miles in every direction, a place called Earth. This is *my* planet, *my* home. I, Cro-Magnon, belong here.

Am I a part of this world? Absolutely. I breathe its air. Its water passes through me. I am made of the same elements that constitute every other creature here: carbon, oxygen, hydrogen, etc. My body metabolizes food into energy and creates new cells, as every body here does. My gut is inhabited by the planet's microbes. But more importantly, I am a fully cognizant animal, aware of who/what I am. I am a human. And when I'm alone in the bush, I feel as wild and free as any fully human being can feel.

Leaving the Alaskan bush was just as much of a shock as entering it. In Juneau there was all kinds of noise and traffic, and people rushing back and forth everywhere. I had to pay cash for a hotel room since the plastic card I had intended to use to do that wasn't working properly. Consequently, I traded in my gun for the coin of the realm. Everywhere I went there were rules, rules, rules – some of them written, most unwritten. I heard the loud buzz of a plane passing overhead and wished I were on it, headed back to the bush, back to that harsh yet beautiful place where everything makes a lot more sense. Yet I was glad I hadn't disappeared into it. I was glad to be among my own kind again. And a couple days later, I was really glad to be back in Judy's arms.

There are discrepancies between what the bush teaches and the way we live our lives in cities, towns and the gentle landscapes surrounding them. Terrible discrepancies. Why is this? What is it about our manmade structures and complex societies that make it so difficult for us to stay connected to our wild selves? How did we become so alienated from nature, from our organic, earthbound past? Coming out of the bush, the tension I felt in the developed places was palpable. The struggle to survive has taken on new meaning here. More to the point, it's as if each and every one of us is at war with ourselves – our wild selves at odds with our civilized selves. Does it have to be this way? Are wildness and civilization mutually exclusive? Do we have to give up the former in order to have the latter?

10. Becoming Civilized

The remnant bones of our distant ancestors, along with the human genome, strongly support what became apparent to me when I was in the Alaskan bush: we human beings are as much a part of the natural world as any other creature. We have evolved on this planet from simple hominids, akin to chimpanzees and the other great apes, to highly cognizant, abstract-thinking and self-aware creatures. We call our species *Homo sapiens* and identify with those who looked just like us and walked the earth sixty thousand years ago.

Those we call Cro-Magnons were humans as much like us behaviorally as they were physically. They engaged in symbolic and ritualistic behavior, spoke a sophisticated language, planned, organized and thought abstractly as we do. They were human in every sense of the word. There's one big difference between them and us, though. Cro-Magnons lived in small bands and subsisted exclusively by hunting and gathering like all the hominins before them, while we live in cities, towns and their hinterlands, subsisting upon domesticated plants and animals.

There are still people living today as hunter-gatherers in New Guinea, the Amazon rainforest, and other remote corners of the world, but they are the exceptions to the rule. The vast majority of us living today inhabit developed places, mostly in or near cities and towns. We are *civil-ized*, therefore dependent upon cities and the cultivated fields around them. The fact that a few so-called primitive people still subsist these days by hunting and gathering only shows that it doesn't have to be this way. We don't have to be *civilized*. And that begs the question: What's the advantage in it?

No doubt our Cro-Magnon ancestors lived close to the earth. They knew the natural world quite well. They had to know it in order to survive. They roamed the wild to get their food, and that in turn kept them wild to some extent. I on the other hand sit indoors tapping away at a keyboard, creating symbols on a screen that eventually convert into the coin of the realm that I use to buy food that has been cultivated, harvested, processed and stored by others. In other words, what I do is highly civilized. Does that make me any less wild? In some ways it does; in other ways it doesn't.

Like all creatures, human or otherwise, I was born wild. But as a child I learned the rules – the acceptable modes of behavior. My parents and teachers, along with the other adults in my life, taught me these rules. Had I been born into a hunter-gatherer society in some remote corner of the world, no doubt I would have grown up learning an entirely different set of rules. But I would have learned rules all the same. Every society has them. The more sophisticated the society, the more rules there are, but even the most primitive society cannot exist without them. Societies are held together by rules. No doubt the Cro-Magnons had their rules. With all the symbols they invented, how could it have been otherwise?

Rules are the laws, customs and etiquette that constitute any given culture. They make efficient social interaction possible. As the anthropologist Leslie White wrote in *The Evolution of Culture*: "A person whose behavior is unpredictable is potentially dangerous." Wild behavior is unpredictable behavior to be sure. "If we are to have normal social intercourse," White goes on to say, "We must be able to predict the behavior of our fellows and they must be able to predict ours." That's where the rules, both written and unwritten, come into play.

Yet a streak of wildness remains in all of us. The rules keep our wildness in check, but it is there all the same. Spend a few days alone in a sprawling forest, mountain or desert wilderness and you will most likely start to feel that wildness emerge from somewhere deep within you. Beyond the reach of society, the rules lose their relevance. What good are rules if there's only you and raw nature, when there's no one else around? Even when I embrace some kind of wilderness ethic such as "leave no trace," I do so with the assumption that someone else will eventually come along to notice. But if I were alone on this planet, an ethic of this sort would be utterly meaningless.

With this in mind, we can surmise that even Cro-Magnons, living as close to nature as they did, still kept their wildness in check to some extent. They had to in order to keep their small bands and simple societies intact. The artifacts they left behind confirm this, as their communal living arrangements do. But in wildness there is freedom to think, say and do whatever one desires. So again we have to ask ourselves: why become *civil-ized* and therefore restricted by rules and more rules? What's the real advantage in it?

Food security. The first tentative steps towards civilization began with food security, with devising ways to exist beyond the limitations of hunting. After all, hunting can be good some years and not so good in others. Animals are relatively rare in this world; plants are abundant. Animals move around; plants do not. So it made sense for prehistoric hunters to establish their camps near places where edible plants grew. Gathering is the fail-safe of hunter-gatherer societies. The next step was to help those plants thrive, what the contemporary archeologist Christine Hastorf calls "plant nurturing." This was something probably done by women, while the men were out hunting. Hastorf theorizes that women often cared for wild edibles close to camp the same way that they cared for their children. This makes sense, and archeological findings at Abu Hureyra and places like it throughout the Near East suggest as much.

The Natufians, who inhabited the Near East towards the end of the Ice Age, were the first known people to experiment with plant domestication. Along with hunting gazelles, they gathered nuts by the basket and used sickles to collect wild cereals. They lived in semi-permanent settlements at a time when temperatures were relatively mild and rain was abundant. As Steven Mithian reports in his book, *After the Ice*: "The sedentary hunter-gatherers at 'Ain

Mallaha, Abu Hureyra and indeed throughout western Asia between 12,500 and 11,000 BC were enjoying the good life." They had plenty of food and, as a consequence, their population grew. "In light of the permanence of their settlements, the many mouths needing to be fed, and the abundance of grinding stones, pestles and mortars," Mithen says, "Wild plants appear to have been managed in a way that we would recognize as cultivation." But it didn't last. The Younger Dryas, a shift back to a cold, dry climate for over a thousand years, put intense pressure on the Natufians. As a consequence their first attempts at agriculture, and the semi-permanent settlements that went with it, were abandoned. The Natufians resorted back to their old ways.

Around 9,500 BC, the Younger Dryas came to an end, along with the summer droughts that it caused. "History repeated itself and sedentary village life was reborn," Mithen reports. Jericho, the earliest known permanently settled town, was founded along with other towns scattered across the Near East. The deliberate, large-scale cultivation of plants took off. This was the beginning of the Neolithic Period, or New Stone Age, in contrast to the Paleolithic or Old Stone Age that we associate with Cro-Magnon culture.

The rise of towns was a great leap forward in terms of food security and social organization. This phase of human history is sometimes called the Neolithic Revolution. It marks the transition between a nomadic, hunting-gathering way of life and a sedentary, agriculturally based one. This sea change took place in the Levant, spreading throughout the Fertile Crescent, from the Nile River in Egypt to the Tigris-Euphrates

Rivers in modern day Iraq. This change also took place in Hindus Valley of India, and along the Yellow and Yangzi Rivers of China. In due time, it took place in the Americas. The change was so pervasive that one is tempted to say it was inevitable. But was it?

Colin Tudge, the author of a slender volume called *Neanderthals, Bandits and Farmers*, argues that the agricultural revolution took place not because it was necessarily an easier or better way to live, but because farmers became the victims of their own success. "Farmers find themselves in a vicious spiral. The more they farm, the more their population rises and the more they are obliged to farm." Maybe so, but isn't that what biological success is all about? According to the book of Genesis in the Bible, God said: "Be fruitful and multiply." Was that a blessing or a curse?

Town and country. We think of them as opposites but they actually go hand in hand. With the widespread practice of agriculture came the rise of towns and cities. The English word "civilization" comes from the Latin word "civilis," which means civil, and is closely related to the word "civitas" which means city. City, civil, civilized. The inference here is clear. Cities are the hubs of civilization and everything civil. The surrounding cultivated lands are merely extensions of them.

Beyond civilization lies barbarism and chaos, or so we are led to believe. Beyond civilization there is only wilderness and all the wild people, plants and animals that inhabit it. What place is there in civilization for wildness of any sort? If you are civilized, you have it burned into your brain that all good things are civil, and that wild behavior at best is a temporary letting go, and at worst a threat to all the things that we hold dear.

Time and time again we are told that wildness and civilization are worlds apart, yet being fully human predates civilization by tens of thousands of years. Even if we dismiss those *anatomically* modern humans living 150,000 years ago as hominids who were not quite like us, we remain fundamentally the same as those *behaviorally* modern humans, Cro-Magnons, who painted on rock walls long before the end of the Ice Age. Cro-Magnons were strictly hunter-gatherers, but a hunter-gatherer is no less human than an agriculturalist or a city-dweller. The prejudice is there all the same, built into our self-congratulatory notions of what it means to be civilized. The wildness of our distant and not-so-distant hunting and gathering kin has no place in our highly sophisticated, highly technological, civilized world, does it? Cro-Magnons would not fit into society today. For one thing they wouldn't understand why we have so many rules, would they?

Jericho, the first permanently settled town, came into existence around 8,000 BC. That was the beginning of civilization, as we know it – the beginning of an increasingly urban existence dependent upon domesticated plants and animals. But Annie Dillard put it all in perspective when she wrote: "We are only about three hundred generations from ten thousand years ago." This we should consider. We know that we humans were nomadic hunter-gatherers for tens of thousands of years *before* we were agriculturalists and urbanites. We also know that our species, *Homo sapiens*, has been around much longer than that. We are wild by nature, yet being civilized is a relatively new thing for us.

The human population has rapidly increased as a consequence of civilization. That's proof positive of our tremendous biological success. Progress! Just think how much easier and better life is now than it used to be. The majority of people living in the world today have longer, healthier lives than both our distant and not-so-distant ancestors. Regardless how we define being fully human, aren't the many benefits of civilization worth the abandonment of our innate wildness?

11. The March of Civilization

Across the Anatolian highlands, in what is now Turkey, archeologists have excavated a cluster of very old Neolithic settlements. Some of these settlements date back to the founding of Jericho and other similar towns in the Levant. At Nevali Çori, Çatal Hüyük, Çayönü Tepesi, and other such settlements, we find the beginning of agriculture, animal husbandry, and the first hints of civilization. In due time, these Neolithc peoples migrated into the Tigris-Euphrates River Valley and established bona fide cities. Uruk, a Sumerian city with a population estimated at 15,000 people in 3,700 BC, was one of the first of them.

Uruk reached its height around 2,800 BC with a population of nearly 80,000 people. Around that time it was ruled by the legendary king, Gilgamesh – a demigod who walled the city, densely packing its inhabitants into an area a little over two square miles. The nearby city Eridu, home of Enki and the other Sumerian gods, supposedly dates back to 5,700 BC, but it never grew to the extent that Uruk did. Besides, Uruk is where Sumerian pictographs gradually developed into the first system of writing, cuneiform. With writing came the codification of laws and, as a result, civilization as we know it.

"Simple cultures normally belong to small societies and complex ones to large," Elman Service states in his book *Origins of the State and Civilization*. This is not news to those of us living today, obliged as we are to fill out tax returns along with countless other forms. How much easier it must have been, a thousand years ago, to pay a tithe to the church and/or state. We can only imagine how simple life must have been five thousand years ago. Things certainly have become more complicated over time, haven't they? Why is that? Elman adds: "The creation and extension of the authority bureaucracy was also the creation of the ruling class, or aristocracy." Again, this is not news. But in the context of civilization and its rise, this should give us pause. As soon as cities were created, the bulk of humanity was divided into two classes: the governing and the governed. This arrangement came with lots of rules created by the governing class to keep the governed in their place – for their own good, of course. Once again, we have to wonder what real advantage there is in this arrangement for the vast majority of us. Food security, right? Or was something else at stake once the city walls went up?

The anthropologist Leslie White believed that the Agricultural Revolution was the first great cultural change, and that we became landowners as a consequence of it. In *The Evolution of Culture* he wrote: "Social organization was transformed from tribal society, based upon kinship, to civil society organized upon the basis of property relations." That sounds about right. You can't own much if you are always on the move, but stay put for a while and the earth beneath your feet becomes valuable. Real estate – who owns it and why? That's a big issue for sedentary folk.

Civilizations cropped up in China, the Indus Valley, the Andes of South America, and Mesoamerica not long after they emerged in the Fertile Crescent – that swath of arable land stretching from Egypt, through the Levant, to Mesopotamia. In Mesopotamia in particular, conditions were ideal for the domestication of plants and animals. That's why those peoples civilized first, and why all hell broke out there before it did anywhere else. As the geographer and historian Jared Diamond observes: "The peoples of areas with a head start on food production gained a head start on the path leading to guns, germs and steel." In his book by that name, *Guns, Germs, and Steel*, Jared argues that civilized peoples overwhelm other peoples by those three means. Armaments, the spreading of diseases that inevitably arise in the tight living quarters of cities, and advanced technology enable one group of people to steamroll another. It's called conquest, and while the reasons justifying it may vary, war or the threat of it is always an essential part of the process.

Around 2,300 BC, Sargon of Akkad conquered most of the Sumerian city-states in Mesopotamia, thus creating the first known empire in the world. War in Mesopotamia was not new. The borders between Sumerian city-states were a constant source of conflict. But Sargon was the first king to create a standing army, conquer one city-state after another, and assume lordship over all the people he conquered. He would certainly not be the last, as this pattern would play itself out time and time again in emerging civilizations throughout the world. Property ownership arises from agriculture, it seems, and eventually leads to conquest. Never mind that none of this makes any sense to those living in hunter-gather societies. To civilized people, conquest and ownership both make perfect sense.

This is not to say that pre-civilized people lived in peace and harmony. On the contrary, there is evidence that the roots of violence reach deep into our past. Steven Mithen reports in his book, *After the Ice,* what scientists found at an archeological site in Egypt dating back at least 11,000 years: "Of fifty-nine people buried in the graveyard, twenty-four had clearly suffered a violent death due to the presence of embedded arrow points and severe cut-marks on their bones and skulls." So civilized people didn't invent war, they merely perfected it. Conquest is simply war on a large, highly organized scale. And it's meant to change things in a major way – winner take all. Land is usually the main thing at stake.

What precipitates conquest? Clearly there can't be conquest without something worth taking, but another civilizing factor is a necessary precondition. There has to be some kind of hierarchy. That comes naturally with the creation of a town or city, where there exists the governing, someone to enforce the will of the governing, and the governed. In other words, a society divided into priest-kings, soldiers, and the peasants working the land. Add to this the officials, merchants, and artisans that naturally arise from the tendency of a civilizing people to specialize and you have the beginning of a caste, or class society. Add to this the slaves that are so often the fruits of conquest, and the picture is complete. Despite what Marxists and other such dreamers would have us believe, there has never been a classless society – not in the civilized world – nor is it likely there ever will be one. Social stratification is an integral part of civilization, rooted in social status, wealth, religion, ideology and, most importantly, the concentration of power into the hands of a few. History shows, time and time again, that war and conquest arise from that. And the elites, those who benefit the most from it, always want more.

Does it have to be this way? Curiously enough, the early Neolithic settlement Çatal Hüyük showed no signs of hierarchy. No temple, no priest-king, or no trappings of the kind of social stratification commonly found in other Neolithic settlements. Walter Fairservice ran with this in this book, *The Threshold of Civilization*, saying: "There is nothing in the evidence so far unearthed at Çatal Hüyük to demonstrate anything else than a cohesive and flourishing mutuality of the kind found wherever primitive man has flourished." So perhaps there is hope for us yet. Perhaps there is a way to organize a society without class, caste or hierarchy. But that isn't going to be easy. Collectively speaking, we have over 5,000 years of bad habits to overcome, and in every civilization there is always *someone* in charge.

In the wild, human beings engage in a struggle to survive as all creatures do. Sustenance is the primary concern. In all the civilized parts of the world – which is nearly everywhere these days – this struggle is more of one group of people against each other. Civilization seems to progress at the tip of a spear, though it is often hidden behind gold or some other measure of value. And there are always winners and losers. Empires come and go, but always there are the masses and the elite who govern them. Regardless what happens to the masses, the elite always seem to benefit from this arrangement. This is as true in Africa, Europe, Asia or the Americas today as it was in the Fertile Crescent 5,000 years ago.

Kings, slaves and everyone between them. The Haves and the Have-nots. Hierarchy, inequality, domination and bloodshed – the history of civilization is rife with it. There are those who believe that this is the way things should be. Nowadays we call them Social Darwinists. They reason that the struggle between human beings is a natural extension of the struggle for survival. It's a dog-eat-dog world, they say, so there will always be winners and losers. More to the point, they believe that the strong have every right to dominate the weak. Oh, but listen to them cry foul the day *they* lose a war! Listen to them scream for the police the moment *they* get robbed. Listen to them whine about how the game is rigged when all their wealth suddenly vanishes in a sudden shift of the economic winds. Social Darwinists are poor losers, believing as they do that everything is as it should be only when they are on top.

More to the point, it doesn't follow that the struggle for existence in nature justifies the kind of things that human beings do to each other. Back when we were all hunter-gatherers, the name of the game was simple: stay alive. That required a great deal of ingenuity and effort, yes, but getting the upper hand in dealings with other humans wasn't at the top of the agenda, if it was on the agenda at all. Oh sure, there must have been spats over hunting grounds back in the day, but there was so much land and so few people 15,000 years ago that one band rarely came into contact with another. Besides, they couldn't risk losing even a few valuable hunters in armed conflict. No, fighting over resources is what we civilized people do, because there are so damned many of us that the sacrifice of thousands, even millions, to the gods of war is no big deal.

In some sense the march of civilization over the millennia has been a biological success story. There weren't more than a few million people in the world during the Old Stone Age, before agriculture took off. Now look at us. We're in the billions! But with this success has come a plethora of problems.

What again are the benefits of civilization? Food security. That's the main thing. That's how it all got started, but soon being civilized became much more than that. With sedentary living came the advantage of a permanent place to get out of the rain. Houses are better places to live than huts or lean-tos. Once you have a permanent place, you can accumulate things: furniture, kitchenware, clothes, jewelry, etc. You can sleep in a comfy bed. In any civilization worthy of the name, there is good sanitation, indoor plumbing, baths, and clean drinking water. Elementary schools are a big plus. Higher education is even better. Then there are the arts, both entertaining and edifying. In more recent times, there is advanced medicine to keep us all happy and healthy well into old age. On top of all that there's security – knowing that soldiers, policemen, and the other enforcers of the rules are there to protect you and your way of life.

Most people spending time in a truly civilized place soon grow to like it. What's there not to like? In such a place people are, as a general rule, happy and healthy. But this comes at a price. Everyone has to contribute something. We all have to work for our daily bread. We have to pay for the privilege of living within the city walls and gaining the protection of The Powers That Be. That's called taxes. We have to pay for the place where we live. That's called rent or a mortgage. And so on. We become indebted to each other, to society at large. This is as true today as it ever was, perhaps even more so. Why is this? According to David Graeber, debt is what civilization is all about. In his book *Debt: the First 5,000 Years*, he puts it right out there: "If we have become a debt society, it is because the legacy of war, conquest and slavery has never completely gone away." This is a concept that is difficult to fully grasp, unless one happens to be one of the Have-nots. To them it's quite clear what the cost of living in the civilized world really is.

The German philosopher Jürgen Habermas looks at civilization in a different way. "Only with the transition to societies organized around a state," he wrote, "Do mythological world views also take on the legitimation of structures of domination." Habermas sees these "mythological world views" as transitional – as something between the magical-animistic worldview of Paleolithic peoples and the more developed civilizations that embrace philosophies and organized religions. *The Epic of Gilgamesh*, a myth that was a pillar of Sumerian society, fits nicely into this way of looking at things. This also explains the shift in ancient Greece from the founding myths of Homer – *The Iliad* and *The Odyssey* – to the more sophisticated worldviews of Plato and Aristotle. But Habermas misses one salient fact: people like their myths, and they embrace them to this day. That's how the "structures of domination" are legitimized. Different cultures have different myths, but always there are myths behind it all.

The great myth of Western civilization goes something like this: life was good when the Mediterranean was a Greco-Roman lake, but it all came apart in the second to fifth centuries due to moral decay and barbarian invasion. Then Christianity saved the day by humanizing the barbarians, thus creating the noble kingdoms that morphed into the modern European states that rediscovered science and reason, opened up the world to free trade, then enlightened otherwise ignorant peoples both at home and abroad. That last step was made famous, of course, by Rudyard Kipling in his poem, "The White Man's Burden." Yes sir, mythological justifications for the conquest of one group of people by another can be very elaborate, indeed.

What are we to make of all this? First and foremost, it becomes crystal clear to anyone with only a cursory understanding of world history that inequality abounds. Not everyone in any given civilization reaps all the benefits of that civilization. On the contrary, most people most of the time are slaves, peasants, or the working poor, barely getting by while a precious few enjoy everything that civilization has to offer. Some of those barely getting by don't even enjoy food security. And when one civilization clashes with another, a lot of people suffer, die, become refugees or slaves – most of them from the lower classes. Not a pretty picture. It makes a wild man like myself seriously question the efficacy of civilization itself. If a civilization can't even guarantee that every belly stays full then what good is it? Food security was, after all, the primary reason why we became civilized in the first place. Perhaps we were better off as hunter-gatherers.

The past 5,000 years of human history has been a litany of war, conquest and domination, with a dose of hatred thrown in for good measure. A fellow named Jesus came along preaching brotherly love and we nailed him to a cross. That should tell us something about ourselves. Us versus Them. Seems like it always comes down to that. We can always find scapegoats for the shortcomings in our societies, but the truth is we have only ourselves to blame. Meanwhile, our population keeps growing and natural resources dwindle, making it that much more difficult for us to get along with each other.

As the theologian Abraham Heschel put it so well: "The chief problem of man is not his nature but what he does with his nature." A human being is a complex creature, neither god nor animal yet somehow both. A human being is neither an angel nor a devil, yet runs the full spectrum of moral possibility. Consequently, civilization is only as good or bad as we make it. Some strides towards a society that works for everyone have been made over time, no doubt. A constitutionally based republic that gives its citizens some say in their governance is far better than an autocratic kingdom where heads roll at the slightest hint of dissent. As a wild man, there's no doubt in my mind which of those two worlds I'd rather inhabit, anyhow. But not everyone concurs. Some still believe that it's a dog-eat-dog world, and if you can cheat your fellow man out of all the benefits of any given society, well, then more power to you. Consequently, civilization remains a less than ideal arrangement for the vast majority of people, making a wild man like myself wonder if it's really worth it.

12. Savage or Civilized?

The word "savage" is emotionally charged. Once uttered, images of men (usually men, not women) engaging in diabolical acts spring to mind: burning, raping, maiming, pillaging, torturing and killing with reckless abandon. Savages are ignorant, thoughtless and out of control. They are superstitious, childlike and impulsive. They are godless and unreasonable. They are the bane of all things humane, cultured and civilized. All this from a single word. Back in the days when Rome and other ancient civilizations flourished, the word "barbarian" carried the same weight. But nowadays we prefer "savage," which stems from the Old French word "sauvage" meaning wild, undomesticated, untamed. The inference here is crystal clear. A wild man is an unsavory character, to say the least.

When I call myself a wild man, most people feel inclined to correct me. After all, wild men do not read, write, engage in civil discourse, or follow society's rules as I do. If a crude, obnoxious, stinky, tattooed, gun-toting drug dealer rolls up on a noisy motorcycle and calls himself a wild man, then most people believe it. After all, he fits the barbarian stereotype. He's the savage. He's the threat to civilization, to humanity, to all we hold dear. See how this works? A prejudice against wildness is hardwired into our civilized way of looking at things. Savagery is everything that is wrong with the world in general, with humankind in particular. That someone could be both wild and fully human, well, that's unthinkable.

Humanity progressed by leaps and bounds, it is widely believed, once we became civilized. It's okay to conquer pre-civilized peoples – savages, that is – because they are supposedly humanized in the process. All imperialists convince themselves of this, regardless of gender, race, culture or creed. Kipling's "White Man's Burden" is a perfect example of this way of looking at things, and how the so-called Christian nations of Western Europe were able to justify their exploitation of the rest of the world for five hundred years. In reality, a great deal of what passes for civilization can be summed up as such: wealthy people making themselves even wealthier at the expense of others. And it's okay, we are told, because *they* are savages and *we* are not.

In the 19th Century, an Italian physician named Cesare Lombroso invented the pseudo-science of "criminal anthropology," based on the notion that some men are born criminals. Stephen Jay Gould gives us a good account of Lambroso and his theory in *The Mismeasure of Man*. According to Lombroso, we can identify criminals by their anatomy. If they are apish looking, they are probably more inclined to criminality. But Gould took issue with this. He noted that "physical apishness can explain a man's barbaric behavior only if the natural inclinations of savages and lower animals are criminal." Good point. Unless wildness and evil are one in the same, Lombroso's theory falls apart.

Lombroso saw the criminal as a savage and, at the same time, as someone morally degenerate. This, he claimed, could be determined simply by looking at a man. Nowadays we might find this notion laughable, but we too have our yardsticks. "We live in a more subtle century," Gould goes on to say, where "the signs of innate criminality are no longer sought in stigmata of gross anatomy, but in twentieth-century criteria: genes and [the] fine structure of the brain." In other words, a deep-seated prejudice against wildness still exists, only now it's justified by genetics.

The moment we call non-civilized or pre-civilized peoples savages, we not only dehumanize those people, but we also rule out the possibility of anyone ever being both wild and fully human. This is the fundamental assumption made by the vast majority of civilized people most of the time. It is so ingrained in the civilized way of thinking that we find it difficult to look upon hunter-gatherer societies, past or present, without a sense of moral superiority. This is similar to the way we look at other creatures on the planet: they are animals and we are something better. We look at hunter-gatherers and say: they are savages and we are something better. And whenever we spotlight the truly evil people among us, we say that they are not worthy of being called civilized. The trouble with them, evidently, is that they have reverted to their savage roots. What other explanation could there be for the evil they do?

When I look at paintings like those found in the Chauvet cave in southern France, I see myself in their Cro-Magnon creators: fully cognizant, abstract-thinking people expressing themselves much the same way I do. But not everyone agrees with me about this. In his book *Before the Dawn*, Nicholas Wade wrote: "The natural assumption is that only people like ourselves could create such appealing works of art. But it is also possible that these are works of a savage intelligence that saw the world with the same visual system and a profoundly different mind." I find this comment deeply disturbing on two counts. First, Wade assumes that the merit of cave art rests in its "appeal," as if our aesthetic judgment of it was the only thing coming into play here. Secondly, Wade suggests that Cro-Magnons had a "savage intelligence" profoundly different from our own. Speak for yourself, Mr. Wade. I am certain that if he and I ever discussed the matter while tramping together through a wild forest for a week, he would find in me hints of that savage intelligence. I do not believe that we civilized folk are as far removed from our Cro-Magnon ancestors as Mr. Wade thinks we are.

The anthropologist Alan Barnard sees things differently. "Universal kinship is found mainly among hunter-gatherers, where it is the norm," he states. This is a belief common among contemporary anthropologists. Hunter-gatherer societies often see all human beings as kin, either immediate or distant. But it's a different story in our sedentary, agriculturally based societies. In civilization it's Us versus Them. Seems like the more civilized we are, the more that kinship diminishes, along with a sense of connectedness to the natural world. "Natural humanity" is what Barnard calls it, and that's what we left behind when we started domesticating ourselves. But we should be careful about jumping to conclusions here. Barnard's view sounds a lot like the idea of the "noble savage" promoted by people like Rousseau a couple hundred years ago. We should guard against idealizing primitive or pre-civilized peoples, and therefore seeing them as morally superior to civilized people. That's just as bad as putting civilized people on a pedestal.

"Savage" is what we call that hardscrabble existence before we became civilized, and that says it all. Humankind is so much better off today than it was 15,000 years ago, isn't it? We have science, reason, modern medicine, the high arts, constitutional governments, social nets for the needy, and thriving economies, not to mention countless technological advantages making transportation and communication so much easier. In addition to all that there are the many conveniences of modern living. Collectively speaking, we are much better off now than we were as Cro-Magnons. But are we better people because of civilization, more righteous or moral? If we take the word "savage" seriously, which is necessary in any discussion of human wildness, we must address this issue. I contend that we are not more decent human beings than our Cro-Magnon ancestors. On the contrary, advanced technology and the machinations of civilization enable the worst among us to do things far more horrific than anything our ancestors could have imagined.

Prehistoric warfare was posturing and threats for the most part. It couldn't have gone far beyond that because small bands of hunter-gatherers can't afford to lose their hunters. When war broke out between our distant ancestors, it was brutal and bloody to be sure, but child's play compared to what we can do today. In the 20th century, when our population swelled into the billions, the situation radically changed. Then humankind could afford total war. During the First World War poison gas, machine guns, and heavy artillery all worked to devastating effect, killing and maiming millions of soldiers. During the Second World War we figured out how to kill and maim people on an even larger scale, soldiers and civilians alike, with scourge-the-earth policies and tons of bombs dropped from planes. Firebombs turned cities into rubble, displacing millions so that starvation, disease and exposure took their tolls long after the bombs exploded. Then came nuclear weapons, biological weapons, intercontinental missiles, napalm, gatling guns, and drones. And none of this would be possible without a vast military-industrial complex behind it all – what only civilization can provide.

But it's not just about technology. Sometimes the greatest horrors we are capable of devising are the direct result of high levels of organization and planning. In the middle of World War Two, the Nazis devised an incredibly efficient way of getting rid of Jews and other undesirables. In retrospect, we call this the Holocaust. The Nazis called it the Final Solution, being the highly effective problem solvers that they were. They exterminated over eleven million people by gas and other means before the end of the war, and would have gone a lot farther with their program had they been given half a chance.

The savagery of modern war greatly surpasses anything a so-called savage could ever do. And it is practiced by the most advanced, industrialized nations on earth. "Everything we had suspected about the most inhuman within the human," the political philosopher Bernard-Henri Lévy recently wrote, "That, in fact, is the truth of war." Some people are so repulsed by modern war that they advocate pacifism. They believe that evil can be eliminated, or at least greatly reduced, simply by doing away with armed conflict. But sinister folks like those with their Final Solutions are not so easily swayed. Only brute force can stop them. Therein lies the great tragedy of the human condition in these modern times: to combat inhumanity, we must fight using whatever means available. So don't blame pre-civilized people for all the evil in the world. Only a highly civilized person could entertain a notion as patently absurd as this.

It is time to rethink what it means to be human and what our relationship is to the world around us. It is time for us to abandon simplistic notions like "savage" and get a real fix on human wildness. It is time to take a long, hard look at civilization as we know it and assess its strengths and weaknesses, its benefits and shortcomings. The confusion that persists between being human and being civilized does not serve us well. We are human because we live in the world, not because we live in cities or their developed environs. The best and worst aspects of humanity are much the same today as they were 15,000 years ago. We won't be able to truly progress as a species, beyond mere biological or material success, until we get a handle on the serious threats that we pose to ourselves. We won't be able to truly prosper until we can find a way of living with each other that is mutually beneficial. Tall order, indeed, but if we do not aspire to this then we as fully human beings will eventually go the way of the dinosaur.

The big question is: where to begin? The answer to this is the same now that it has always been. Change begins within us, within each and every one of us. To facilitate this change, it helps to go to a place where the cacophony of civilization is greatly reduced – to a wild place. There it is possible to gain perspective, to see ourselves for what we really are.

13. The Tonic of Wilderness

Civilization leapt forward in the late 18th and early 19th centuries with the advent of steam, the use of machines, and rise of the factory system. It started in Great Britain, quickly spread through Europe and the United States, and eventually swept through the rest of the world. With it came improvements in living standards and food production that turned a billion people into eight billion in a little more than two hundred years. Commonly known as the Industrial Revolution, this rapid change in the way humankind does things can only be compared to the Agricultural Revolution, which took place at the very dawn of civilization. In a sense the Industrial Revolution is proof positive of humankind's continued biological success, for we have done what no other creature on this planet could possibly do. We have altered our relationship to nature so profoundly that instead of it being a place in which we must survive, it has become a wellspring of raw materials to be tapped. This, in turn, is having a profound effect upon how we see ourselves as human beings.

Before the Industrial Revolution, the word

"wilderness" referred to hostile places beyond the reach of civilization, largely unexplored and undeveloped. The wilderness was where a few hunter-gatherers scratched out a marginal existence for themselves, or they were places not populated at all. In ancient times, the wilderness was a desert wasteland where holy men went for divine inspiration. During the Middle Ages it was a frightful forest, or an unknown expanse of land or sea. Four hundred years ago wilderness was a wide-open landscape, where desperate folk went to start new lives for themselves, when the crowded cites, wars and famines of the old country became too much to bear. But people started looking at wilderness in an entirely different way once there was little of it left. This was especially true in the United States in the mid-19th century, when the vast forests started disappearing fast, at a time when people were starting to feel the stresses of industrialization.

"From the forests and wilderness come the tonics and barks which brace mankind," the woods wanderer Henry David Thoreau wrote. Even though he was something of an outsider in his day, as woods wanderers usually are, his "tonic of wilderness" soon became a battle cry for those who sensed that industrialization was taking its toll on humankind. What is gained? What is lost? Those who firmly believed that technology solves everything still saw wild places as merely obstacles to human progress. It had to be tamed in order to make room for civilization. But Thoreau saw things differently. "In Wildness is the preservation of the World," he said in no uncertain terms. Not wilderness per se, but *wildness*. This distinction would only be recognized later, once we began to fully realize what is at stake.

With an eye towards Yosemite as well as other wild and beautiful places in the western expanses of the United States, the naturalist John Muir was an early advocate for the preservation of wild places. "The clearest way into the Universe is through a forest wilderness," he wrote, recognizing a direct connection between wild nature and human well being. His advocacy led to the creation of the first national parks. Others soon followed his lead. Theodore Roosevelt protected more wild country than any American president before him or since. The conservationist Aldo Leopold argued for a "land ethic." Along with Bob Marshall, Harvey Broome, Benton MacKaye and a few other lovers of wild places, he founded the Wilderness Society. The tireless efforts of that organization, along with Muir's Sierra Club and other conservationist organizations, prompted the U. S. Congress to pass the Wilderness Act in 1964. That, in turn, led to the creation of designated wilderness areas throughout the nation, thus preserving a portion of remaining wild lands. During the 20th century the preservation movement spread across the planet with the creation of national parks, wildlife preserves and natural world heritage sites everywhere. Oddly enough, it has taken the Industrial Revolution, and the profound impact it has made upon our collective psyche, to awaken in us the vital importance of humankind's connection to the natural world.

What exactly does a wilderness provide that we can't find elsewhere? As someone who has spent considerable time alone in wild places during the past forty-odd years, I still find its tonic difficult to articulate. Early in the 19th century, Romantic writers referred to the combined beauty, awe and terror of the wild as the sublime. That comes close. Wilderness is where I go to be humbled, to find my place in the world, to become aware of my creature-ness and ultimately my human-ness. While spending a little time alone in a wild place, all this is possible.

What does wilderness teach us? Holmes Rolston III, who has been called the father of environmental ethics, said it simply in his book, *Philosophy Gone Wild*: "In the wilderness I am reminded of what culture lulls me into forgetting, that I have natural roots." This is easy to forget. After all, we have come a long way since the cave-painting days of our distant ancestors. Civilization is now our frame of reference, not the natural world.

While going about our affairs in the developed lowlands, it is way too easy to slip into the self-congratulatory mindset that plagues all civilized peoples. We are so impressed by our accomplishments – with the great cities we have built, with our vast communication and transportation networks, with our scientific and technological advances, and high arts. We are giddy with a sense of success unrivaled in the natural world. More importantly, we are impressed by the social structures we have created, by the decency and humanity built into the elaborate sets of rules that we have created, both written and unwritten. But all this hubris is rooted in assumptions that come with being civilized. Give the wild half a chance and those assumptions come into question. As Rolston went on to say, "Wilderness is a bizarre place where our conventional values get roughed up. We learn the relatively and subjectivity of what in civilization can seem such basic rules."

In a wild place it is not just the rules that come into question, but the very preconceptions that we have about ourselves. Take for example the notion that humankind is the pinnacle of evolution. When one spends enough time in the wild, one sees how many ingenious ways there are for plants and creatures to survive and prosper. Then how we live is not quite so impressive. When human strife is taken into consideration – grotesque inequality, human suffering, unrelenting conflict, etc. – then what we've accomplished to date is not very impressive at all. After spending enough time in a wild place, one is soon questioning the most fundamental precepts upon which civilization has been built.

But what about this idea we have about wilderness? Is it legitimate? Does wilderness even exist? In the strictest sense, no. If we are talking about a pocket of wild nature completely free from the taint of humanity, then definitely no. *Homo sapiens* has been roaming the world for tens of thousands of years. There are few places where we haven't been, if any at all. More to the point, when we pull ice core samples from glaciers at either one of the poles, or from glaciers in the most remote mountain ranges, we find carbon deposits from our industrialization. Our impact is global. Even as hunter-gatherers, long before civilization, we burned prairies and forest floors to make hunting and gathering easier. More than once I have wandered off-trail in a so-called wilderness area and stumbled upon the remains of human industry or the cellar hole of what was once a homestead. If by the word "wilderness" one means a pristine place where no human being has ever left a mark, then no, there is no such thing. There is only an approximation of it.

The contemporary writer William Cronon has taken the idea of wilderness to task. "Far from being the one place on earth that stands apart from humanity," he wrote, "It is quite profoundly a human creation." This is apparent to anyone familiar with the history of the wilderness preservation movement, and why it has arisen. If it weren't for the Wilderness Act of 1964, there would be no designated wilderness areas in the United States, where nature has been legislated by congress to remain "forever wild." This is an ongoing process. Preservationists celebrate the creation of new wilderness areas, or the augmentation of existing ones. So Cronon is right. They are a human creation.

When one thinks about it, it is impossible to have wilderness without civilization. To pre-civilized people, the word "wilderness" has no meaning. To them there are only human beings and the world. And that is why the word "wildness" carries more weight than "wilderness" does. For wildness refers to things in their original state. Wildness is the reality of the world despite all human influence, despite human constructs like cities, towns, cultivated fields, and designated wilderness areas. Wildness is the way things are naturally, including us, despite all domestication. A designated wilderness area merely keeps human influence at bay long enough for nature to do its thing. But it can be radically altered or even destroyed. Wildness itself, on the other hand, is forever.

When I was a teenager, my father often lectured me about the real world and what I had to do to survive in it. The real world about which he spoke is the world of commerce. To survive in it one has to make money. Working to feed oneself goes without saying. We all have to do that, of course. But what my father was really trying to say is that we must pay careful attention to how society is organized in order to take advantage of the opportunities that arise in it and therefore accumulate wealth. In my youth I ran off to wild places to play, to temporarily escape from the "real world" that my father talked about. But, in due time, I learned that the world is more than the sum total of social organizations that we call civilization. Much more. It is everything that exists. Civilization is only a fraction of reality. The natural world, on this planet and spread across the entire universe, is unequivocally wild yet very real. Taking this into account, the naturalist John Hay wrote: "It is not often that we can shed the unending distractions with which we surround ourselves, but when we do the realities appear." And these realities, I believe, are what Thoreau and his peers meant by the tonic of wilderness.

Wild places, be they designated wilderness areas or simply places not yet fully developed, teach us a great deal about ourselves and how we fit into the greater scheme of things. They give us a sense of perspective. Their great silences enable us to think more clearly than we usually do about who/what we are. More often than not, the perspective one gains by a wilderness experience is strictly personal. Sometimes it is only a temporary escape from the hustle and bustle of the developed lowlands – something that enables one to see one's life in new and refreshing ways. But to woods wanderers like myself, who turn to the wild for better understanding of the world at large, there is also the occasional epiphany. These are moments when the many discrepancies between civilized life and the natural world become crystal clear. And that's what enables the wildness within to emerge. Without wild places I fear that humankind will lose all sense of perspective. Then everyone will fall victim to the ridiculous notion that we are gods, thereby forgetting our creature-ness. But for now, it is still possible to prevent that.

14. Escaping to Wild Places

Whenever the hustle and bustle in the developed
lowlands becomes too much, I drop everything and
head for a wild place. Sometimes an hour or two is
enough. Other times I need a couple days in the wild.
Every once in a while, I disappear into deep woods for
a week or more to quash the frustration and despair that
builds up inside me over time. The madness of
civilization, with its frenzied pace, contradictory rules,
conflicting values, mind-boggling systems and inane
bureaucracies, can drive even the most levelheaded
person to the point of distraction. To someone like
myself, it's enough to elicit a primal scream. So I
escape to a wild place where the great silences calm my
nerves, enabling me to think clearly once again. I
imbibe the tonic of wilderness, thus preventing me from
becoming one of those maniacs on the evening news
blowing up buildings in the name of God or country,
killing themselves and others in a fit of moral hysteria,
or otherwise making a big bloody mess of things. The
stresses of living in the modern world affect us all.
How others cope is something of a mystery to me. But
whenever I start feeling the madness of civilization

closing in, I grab my rucksack and head for the hills.

I escape to some wild place, fleeing the developed lowlands like a terrified animal fleeing a forest fire. I know that if I stay too long in my regular workaday routine, the madness will overwhelm me. I escape, yes, I escape to higher ground, where there are no signs telling me where I can and cannot go, no forms to fill out, no television screens, no cameras watching, and nobody telling me what to say, think or do. I escape *from* the madness *to* sanity, from the artificial world created by humans to the natural world.

Alaska ruined me. All it took was a couple weeks alone in the bush to undercut my mindless compliance to society, trashing the belief fixed in my head that the march of civilization is ultimately for the best. I am no anarcho-primitivist. That is, I do not believe that civilization itself is inherently evil and that to save ourselves we must all return to a pre-civilized way of life. That's an absurd notion. Civilization is here to stay, and there is as much right with it as there is wrong. That much said, I find it increasingly more difficult to function in society or believe in the righteousness of it after fending for myself in the Alaskan bush for a while. No doubt I was drawn to wild places before I went to Alaska. I have felt the urge to wildness for as long as I can remember. But after the bush, I can no longer claim to be an utterly civilized man – that and that only. After the bush, wildness has remained firmly lodged in my consciousness and I can't think of a good reason to suppress it. It's too big a part of who/what I am. So now, several decades later, it is crystal clear to me that my humanity and my wildness are inextricably entwined.

Escaping from the madness of civilization for an hour or two is incredibly easy. All I have to do is drive a few miles out of town to the nearest pocket of woods and slip into it for a while. Several days in the wild is a little harder to pull off and requires a longer drive. But my home turf, the Green Mountains, is good for that. Going alone into the wild for a week or more is much more difficult. For starters, it's hard to drop everything and disappear that long. Then there's the challenge of finding in the Northeast a chunk of wild country sprawling enough to accommodate the urge to roam aimlessly for days on end.

Back in '95 I backpacked Vermont's Long Trail, from Massachusetts to Canada, along the spine of the Green Mountains. That was my first extended immersion in the wild after Alaska. Food caches strategically placed along the trail beforehand kept me out of the developed lowlands for a month – road crossings notwithstanding. In 2006 I hiked the Northville/Placid Trail, which arcs through the Adirondacks. That kept me in the wild for two weeks. In 2009 I hiked the 100 Mile Wilderness, a remote section of the Appalachian Trail in north-central Maine. That kept me in the thick of it for twelve days straight. But all three of those outings took place on well maintained trails traveled by scores of hikers – pathways as good for socializing with like-minded others as they are for grooving with nature. Time in the wild, yes, but not quite wild enough for me.

West Canada Lakes Wilderness, located in the southern Adirondacks, has been my favorite place to go since I first went there back in 2002. It's one of the biggest roadless areas east of the Mississippi – a good place to get lost, therefore a great place to go wild. I have gone back there several times since 2002 and haven't been disappointed. Sometimes I hike a portion of the Northville/Placid Trail cutting through that wilderness area then veer away. Other times I follow a less beaten path into it. Occasionally, I step off the marked trails and bushwhack to a remote pond or some other place where deep forest solitude is virtually guaranteed. Always I feel wildness stir within me while I'm out there, and always I return home feeling much more human.

How wild does a place have to be to work its magic? That varies from one person to the next, I suppose. The degree to which the wild affects each one of us varies as well, depending upon one's ability to connect with it. I realize that I'm something of an anomaly. Most people have no desire to go deep into the woods, and they probably have no business being there. Certain skills are required, no doubt. Then there is the matter of risk. Those who have rescued clueless and/or unfortunate hikers warn against going alone into wild places. More importantly, the wild can only work its magic if one is comfortable with it, and that also varies greatly from one person to the next. Much depends upon the nature of any given wild place. For example, while I feel at home in deep woods, I am not comfortable on the open sea, which is just as wild. Others prefer desert expanses that I find absolutely dreadful. Still others are drawn to the stillness and simplicity of arctic landscapes that seem utterly desolate to me. To each his or her own. And regarding the degree of separation from civilization, to each his or her own as well.

How wild does a place have to be to draw out the wildness within? A state park or a wooded hill probably works for some. I'm no judge of such things. All I know is how the wild affects me, and where I have to be for that to happen. From what I've read, there are other people like me who have to go deep in order to be profoundly affected by the wild. From conversations I've had with other woods wanderers, I gather that epiphanies in such places are not uncommon. But one has to be ready for it. Much depends upon one's frame of mind, as well as being in the right place at the right time. And that too varies from one person to the next.

We all escape the madness of civilization one way or another. Some escape into the stories presented in books or on screens, others into video games, still others into drugs and alcohol. Some people withdraw to a quiet room, close their eyes then meditate. Some escape into diversions that might seem silly or deviant to the rest of us. There are innumerable ways to escape the stresses of modern living, but only one way to escape into unadulterated reality. To do that one must venture into a wild place. Only there is nature inescapable. Only there does our *human* nature fully realize itself.

15. Global Civilization

During the past hundred years, humankind has undergone a remarkable transformation. Civilization has gone global, radically changing the way we interact with each other. The various civilizations that have developed on this planet have started merging into one. This was not intentional, nor was it encouraged. And it is a mistake, I think, to see this as either a good or bad thing. It is simply the outcome of mass transportation, mass communication, and the widespread exchange of ideas as well as goods and services.

Global civilization is also the inevitable result of two horrific world wars and the development of nuclear weapons – weapons so devastating that mutually assured destruction (MAD) has forced us into a new world order. Oh sure, there are still plenty of conflicts between human beings, between competing ideologies, religions, cultures, corporations, and nation states. One could argue that there is more conflict now than ever before. Serious discrepancies exist between the Haves and the Have-nots, and the resources on this planet are finite. As a consequence of this, we can't help but step on each other's toes. Still war as it was practiced for

5,000 years – a winner-take-all contest between one empire and another – is pretty much out of the question now. Such a war would be catastrophic for all of us.

The economy is the main thing, and technology serves it. Once humankind went digital, creating computer systems and linking them together into a worldwide web called the Internet, the boundaries between states and cultures started eroding fast. This development was not a frivolous one, and it certainly isn't one that will go away just because some of us resent its intrusion into every aspect of our lives. No, there is too much to be gained by it, too much wealth generated by this system for corporations, governments, various institutions and cold-blooded opportunists to abandon it. A few isolated bands of Luddites may choose to have nothing to do with Internet but it is here to stay, dominating our lives for better or worse.

This does not bode well for the wildness that stirs within. An Orwellian world where everyone is under surveillance and individual freedom is a thing of the past, yes, that's a legitimate concern, but the threat we face today goes deeper than that. Much deeper. Our very humanity is at stake. When it is no longer possible for anyone to get off the grid – even temporarily – how will any of us be able to cultivate a deep and lasting connection with the natural world? What will any of us be then but cogs in a vast, self-perpetuating system divorced from natural reality? To some people this projection into the future may sound like science fiction. To others it is just another complaint about the way thing are. But to a wild man like myself, who has witnessed how profoundly things have changed during the past half century, the loss of our humanity as a consequence of civilization globalizing is a very real threat.

The 21st century is the first century of a globalized civilization, even though it has roots in the 20th. The world we live in now is an infinitely complex matrix of interactions that affects everyone. And with that comes the full spectrum of emotional responses. But if life in this day and age were summed up in one word, it would have to be this: stress. This stress is caused by not really knowing what's going on, having to constantly deal with conflicting values, being told contradictory things, and having to follow rules that make little or no sense. This keeps us all off-balance. This is the madness of civilization that each and every one of us faces, each and every day. It manifests itself on our streets, in our public meeting places, in all of our institutions, and nearly every aspect of our lives. There is a certain irony in this, of course, for we live in the Information Age. One would think that it would be easier now than ever before to know what's going on. But ours is actually the Age of Misinformation.

Never have we had so much access to information nor have we been so much in control of our lives – in theory, anyhow. The problem here is complexity. In an effort to make our lives easier and therefore better, we have made everything incredibly difficult and complicated... therefore easy to distort and disrupt. "Men of today seem to feel more acutely than ever the paradox of their situation," the writer and social critic Simone de Beauvoir wrote three-quarters of a century ago, and it still holds true today. "The more widespread their mastery of the world," she went on to say, "the more they find themselves crushed by uncontrollable forces." Indeed. Welcome to the 21st century, to a time when civilizations are merging into each other, when all our different ways of life are colliding. The resulting chaos is evident in our daily lives. And it is right there on our television screens and other electronic devices for us to see.

I am one of the lucky few who can escape to some wild place whenever the madness of civilization becomes too much to bear. But this does not address the problem for humankind at large. The stresses of life today adversely affect the vast majority of people in innumerable ways: neurosis, psychosis, suicide, the abuse of drugs and alcohol, and every imaginable kind of self-destructive behavior. Whenever these stresses are externalized, they lead to road rage, domestic violence and myriad other forms of social deviance. Sometimes even homicide. When combined with religion, ideology or simple greed, they can lead to crime, terrorism, even civil war. Sometimes all three. Whole societies are imploding from it. Evil is manifesting itself in ways that are all too civilized. So those of us who care about the human condition feel compelled to ask: How do we fix this?

Henri Bergson struck upon the fundamental problem when he wrote: "*Homo sapiens*, the only creature endowed with reason, is also the only creature to pin its existence to things unreasonable." No doubt we are rational creatures embracing irrational ideas. For tens of thousands of years, our ability to think abstractly – the ability to see things not only as they are but as they could be – served us well, enabling us not just to survive but to prosper in the natural world.

Creative thinking and innovation have served us well over the millennia. But now we seem to be the victims of our own success, creating a world so out of touch with the reality of nature that our very humanity has become endangered. This is not a brand new situation by any means. One could argue that it began with civilization itself over 5,000 years ago. All the same, this problem rose to a whole new level when we industrialized. Now that we are in the throes of a digital revolution, with all of us becoming connected in one great, infinitely complex system, we have quite a mess on our hands. Going back to a simpler time and place is not an option – not for humankind as a whole anyhow. So we must fix the errors inherent in civilization itself. To do that, we must identify those errors. Ah, that's where things get tricky.

The world's civilizations grew out of pre-civilized cultures, and those transformations weren't any more premeditated than the recent rise of global civilization was. Things just happened. Someone started planting seeds, someone else started herding goats, someone else built permanent structures, and soon there were towns, city-states, and so on. Still, at every step along the way, people must have asked themselves, either consciously or unconsciously: Is this really working for us? Food security, the primary reason for civilization, came at a price, and that price was the surrender of individual power. Whenever an individual gives his or her power to someone else, to a group, a collective, a tribe, or a city-state, there is always the possibility of that power being abused. It is for the common good, we are told, and that's how the trouble begins. As Bertrand de

Jouvenel pointed out in his seminal work of political philosophy, *On Power*: "As soon as Power is conceived as being exclusively the agent of the common good, it must form a clear picture for itself of what this common good is." And down we go, deep into the morass or morality where people *seriously* disagree with each other.

Clearly the errors inherent in civilization as a whole lie in the way that power is concentrated, and how civilization has been organized as a result. In the beginning it was all about priest-kings, warring kings, then emperors. That was great arrangement for an elite, the so-called nobility, but didn't work out so well for everyone else. Not really. Nobility is gangsterism, where an empowered few force their will upon the rest of us. The rise of constitutionally based governments during the past few hundred years has been a definite improvement, empowering all individuals and not just those belonging to any given elite. Still the errors inherent in civilization persist. Power remains concentrated in the hands of a few at the expense of the many, and this is not a situation that's easily remedied as the shortcomings of so many modern states attest. Wealth and power have a tendency to become concentrated, I should say. In the infinite complexities of global civilization, this more true today than ever before.

The rule of law. In any civilization worthy of the name, law reigns supreme. Therein lies another big problem. Unless those laws are divinely inspired – which is always a questionable prospect – human beings must create them. But, as we all know, human beings are fallible creatures. "What is meant by calling man fallible?" Paul Ricoeur asked, "Essentially this: that the *possibility* of moral evil is inherent in man's constitution." And if "man's constitution" is evil to some extent, then surely any constitution he devises is the same – a flawed document to say the least. Better than having an elite telling us what to do, but flawed all the same. In short, laws are only as good as those who make them.

How is any of this relevant to human wildness? By now it should be obvious to the reader what a wild man like myself makes of all this. I do not obey the law, any law, simply because *it's the law*. Nor do I consider laws or the civilization that depends on them legitimate simply because those who have more power than me say so. The beauty of constitutional government is that it empowers everyone – in theory, anyhow. In reality it might be a different story, as those who wield power are often not held to the same standard as the rest of us. All the same, it's a step in the right direction.

Ultimately, I look at civilization as all wild people do, as all human beings should and ask myself: Is this really working for me? The common good is no good at all unless it addresses the needs of each and every one of us. If civilization fails to do this, then we should be allowed to return to hunting and gathering. This is not the least bit realistic, of course. There are too many of us now.

As global civilization unfolds, replacing all the civilizations that came before it and encompassing every aspect of our lives, the hunting-gathering option is off the table. There simply isn't enough open space for billions of people to live that way, and the few that still do so will eventually be assimilated. We are all fast becoming a part of the global civilization whether we like it or not. But this does not change the fact that we are wild at heart. We human beings were once hunter-gatherers fully immersed in nature, until civilization displaced us. That displacement doesn't change what we are. A deep connection to nature is what ultimately makes us human. Civilization – even one as vast and complex as the one in which we now find ourselves – must somehow accommodate us in this regard. Otherwise what's the point of it?

16. Wildness, Freedom
and Being Human

Wild and free. When it comes to animals, we find it
difficult to utter the first word without inferring the
other. A domesticated animal is not free, nor can a wild
animal remain free once it becomes dependent upon
humans for sustenance or is locked away in a confined
space. That much is obvious. So what about human
beings? What makes us any different? With all the
political talk there is about freedom, how free can we
be within the confines of civilization? Did we not roam
freely through the natural world for tens of thousands of
years? Were we not just as wild then as any other
creature? Were we not lured into domestication by the
promise of food security and the other advantages of
civilized living? Is there no wildness left in us, and if
not, then why all this foolish talk about freedom?

Aldo Leopold, an early advocate for wilderness
preservation, was keenly aware of the necessity of
wide-open spaces. "Of what avail are forty freedoms
without a blank spot on the map?" he asked. That is a
question well worth asking. Mobility is an integral part

of freedom in any real sense – to go wherever one pleases, whenever one chooses to do so. Within the confines of civilization, this is simply not possible. There are restricted places where only authorized personnel can go. There are all kinds of rules about where any given individual can go at any given time. For example, I can't just walk into some corporate headquarters or some government agency and roam about freely. I can't enter a store after business hours, or camp in a city park. Most land belongs to *someone*. If I go on it without permission I am trespassing. But when I'm in a truly wild place – a blank spot on the map – I can go wherever I want, whenever I want. This may not seem important in the greater scheme of things, but the implications of it are profound.

Freedom of thought often accompanies freedom of movement, but does the former require the latter? Mahatma Gandhi once said: "You can chain me, you can torture me, you can even destroy this body, but you will never imprison my mind." While that may be true of the strong-willed among us, most people succumb to social pressure regarding what to think. In fact, neither chains nor torture nor bodily destruction are even necessary. To imprison the minds of most people, all you have to do is keep bombarding them with the same old tired phrases, or better yet, put them in a situation where they cannot imagine things being any other way. That is certainly a form of imprisonment. But let them wander freely in a wild place for a while and some of them just might start thinking differently…

Whenever I wander alone in a wild place, my mind wanders as well. I think about things I would not otherwise think about. I wander, I wonder. I question everything. Once I leave the beaten path, the world opens up to me. Nature teaches me, time and time again, that the world is chock full of possibility. Few things are cut in stone. While wandering in a wild place, my mind slowly goes wild. The more solitary my journey, the faster this happens.

No doubt most people following the trails that pass through wild places carry with them all the mental encumbrances and preconceptions of civilized life. The most obvious of these is goal orientation. A mountain summit is especially good for that. Hordes of hikers flock to mountains, and once the mission of reaching the top is accomplished, they return home largely unaffected by their journey. Their civilized shield never comes down. Even then the wild has an insidious influence on some of them, working its way into their worldview without them even realizing it. Wild places have a way of opening up closed minds, suggesting as they do a world of possibilities. For this reason alone, they should be preserved, set aside from development. Without them it is way too easy to believe that the manmade world is all that really matters, and that the natural world is secondary.

No one with even a remedial grasp of evolution will deny that human beings were once completely immersed in the wild world. Serious disagreement arises only when we look into the past and try to ascertain exactly when and how we lost that deep connection to nature, and what we are now as a consequence. Civilization has changed the way humankind lives, no doubt, with the possible exception of a few tribes of hunter-gathers still hiding in equatorial forests. Eventually civilization will assimilate them as well.

Civilization, the world we have created for ourselves, is something completely different from the wild world, yet it functions within that world. We do not exist in a vacuum. We need the resources of the natural world to live. But that's where we go wrong in our view of nature. When the natural world is seen as nothing more than the sum total of the resources in it, we lose sight of reality, including what we are as human beings. Civilization does not define us, nature does. In that regard, human beings are and always will be just a little bit wild. To create a perfectly domesticated world with no shred of wildness in it, everything in nature would have to be turned into commodities, and humanity itself would have to be quashed, along with all talk about freedom.

In a sense, Gandhi was right. A *wild* mind cannot be imprisoned. But a tame one can be. In fact, that's the definition of the tame mind: imprisoned in a fixed, socially acceptable way of perceiving the world. The wild mind will have no part of that. The wild mind, that is to say the *fully human* mind, will always be capable of thinking something that has never been thought before – that which is neither fixed nor altogether socially acceptable. Therein lies the essence of human freedom. Abstract thinking is what made us human, what freed us from the constrictions of mere survival in the natural world. And it remains our defining attribute.

Civilization is the consequence of abstract thought, yet it comes with its own constrictions – social stratification, grotesque inequalities, and other limitations that are entirely unnecessary. Humankind will have to overcome all this in order to be truly free. That will take time, of course. The more profound a change, the longer it takes. Unfortunately, humankind is moving in the opposite direction these days, towards the consolidation of all cultures into a global civilization, where individuals are but cogs in a vast machine. The possibility of everyone becoming utterly tame and completely subjugated to that machine has never been as strong as it is today.

The wild mind. Protecting that is what freedom is all about. As the French philosopher Henri Bergson pointed out, in the primitive, small societies that existed before civilization, this happened naturally. "Man was designed for very small societies," he wrote, "But we must admit that the original state of mind survives, hidden away beneath the habits without which indeed there would be no civilization." The original state of mind has been suppressed, yes, yet it lives on within us. To a great extent, our wildness has become sublimated. The wild mind is alive and well in all avenues of creative thought: the arts, philosophy, scientific inquiry, innovation of any sort, and every kind of spiritual exploration. One could argue that the wild mind has never been as active as it is today. A visit to the nearest bookstore, art gallery, or museum confirms this. The wild mind always finds a way to express itself.

Some people express their wildness through the clothes they wear, through hairstyles, tattoos, piercings, or other bodily adornments. No doubt our Cro-Magnon ancestors would have approved of this. They adorned themselves as well. Is this modern primitivism or the somewhat socially acceptable attempts of alienated folk to assert their humanity? Those whose minds are tamed do not approve of such adornments. To them anything that upsets the status quo is savage, decadent, evil. Whether they realize it or not, these hopeless conformists are well on their way towards becoming mere cogs in the vast, global machine. In order for that machine to defeat the rest of humanity, all vestiges of wildness must go – anything that smacks of individuality.

The anthropologists are onto this. Claude Lévi-Strauss wrote about the wild or savage mind. Jim Goody wrote about the domestication of it. Dan Sperber clarified the matter by identifying the savage mind as "untamed thought." According to the Alan Barnard, they all agree on one point: "'Untamed thought' is prevalent in the human condition." Barnard sees this as "the natural, creative human understanding that comes from almost any intellectual activity, apart from 'science' in a narrow sense." I don't know what Bernard meant by that "science" disclaimer, but it's clear what he and these other anthropologists are trying to say. The wild mind is an active, untamed way of thinking, and it is as old as humanity itself.

Freedom is an abstract notion. To animals this concept is meaningless – until they encounter humankind that is. When wild animals are captured, their sudden loss of freedom must come as a shock. What a strange feeling it must be to look at the world from behind bars for the very first time! They couldn't have imagined it otherwise. As for domesticated animals, well, what else do they know but domestication? Even my dog, accompanying me on countless excursions into wild forests, doesn't quite grasp the concept of freedom. Yet all human beings know the difference between freedom and bondage. Only when fretting about security, while subject to innumerable laws both written and unwritten, and at the mercy of the almighty dollar do people become as confused about the matter as domesticated animals are. And rightly so. The civilized world is complex and all consuming. There's little room for a person to consider any alternatives while completely immersed in it.

Yet there is always the freedom of wild places for those of us fortunate enough to be able to go there. Then one can think wild thoughts as one rambles through the woods, drinking from streams like any other animal, huddling around a campfire as Cro-Magnons once did, and sleeping beneath the stars. Then freedom goes from being an abstract concept to something very concrete. It stirs within. Then one knows exactly what it *feels* like to be fully human, and the hubbub in the developed lowlands that passes for civilized living doesn't seem so important any more. Then it is enough to simply breathe and be alive in the world – the real world, the world of nature. The big question is: How do we keep the vast, monolithic, global civilization from completely overwhelming us, from robbing us of this vital aspect of our humanity? To know that, we have to know what it is exactly that we are up against.

17. Beyond Human Nature

Wildness is an essential part of being human. Once we are completely divorced from the natural world, we will become something else, something other than human. Some people gleefully anticipate this, thinking that we will become gods – perhaps even immortal – and all the shortcomings of being *naturally* human will be overcome. All we have to do is manipulate the human genome, they say. Then our progeny will be perfect specimens, immune to most if not all diseases and in no way deformed or ugly. Strong, highly intelligent and beautiful, these superhuman creatures will populate other planets and spread across the galaxy – forever and ever, amen! And all the heavy lifting can be done in a laboratory. No need for the messy, unpredictable business of intercourse, pregnancy and the rest of it. Perhaps the messy business of eating and defecating can be done away with, as well. That does, after all, keep us tethered to natural world. To become gods, we must progress beyond nature.

Is this science fiction? It used to be, before the advent of genetic manipulation. Now the only thing holding back the Frankensteins from creating their ideal creatures is a thin veneer of laws buttressed by antiquated values. But values change over time, as history attests. If we could go back in time and tell a conquering people a few thousand years ago that it's wrong to conquer and enslave other people, they would laugh at us. Or a few hundred years ago for that matter. The point here is that we now possess the means to manipulate the human genome, and there's not much to stop the Frankensteins from doing so. Radical changes to what we are as human beings could easily happen. Taking into consideration humankind's ongoing infatuation with technology, these changes probably will happen. The big question is: what will we make of ourselves in the process? Creatures much more civilized than we are today, that's for certain. That's a good thing, if one believes that being civilized and being human are one in the same. But what room will there be for our wildness in all this, for a sustained connection to the natural world? And once we completely sever our connection to nature, will it still make sense to call ourselves human beings?

Genetic manipulation is not the only threat to our collective humanity. There are countless ways in which we can confound ourselves with technology. Once again, it seems, we are becoming victims of our own success, just as we did when we first civilized, and again when we industrialized. Now well into the Digital Age, with every person, every culture and every system being connected, it is hard to imagine future generations slipping off the grid in any way, shape or form. Global civilization is all encompassing, and anyone living beyond its reach is a threat to it – a potentially disruptive force. No, living off the grid won't even be possible a few hundred years from now. We will all be caught in the 'Net, one way or another. Eventually there will be nowhere on this planet to scratch out an existence for oneself completely separated from the all-pervasive global system. And those who still try to do so will be looked upon condescendingly as primitives. That is, after all, the way civilized people think.

According to the mid-20th century essayist, Loren Eiseley, the technological revolution has created a rapidly changing social environment to which we can never fully adjust, and our machines are constantly distracting us from ourselves. As a consequence, "this outward projection of attention... has come dangerously close to bringing into existence a type of man who is not human." This he wrote over half a century ago, *before* the Digital Age got underway, before the Internet, social media, cell phones, video games, and the Global Positioning System. Now a sea change in the way we live – the way in which we interact with each other and the world around us – is taking place. We are fast becoming something quite different from those who lived in the days before computers.

As with all things human, what we *think* about our selves and the world around us lies at the heart of the way in which live. Perception is everything. That is, we live in accordance with how we view the world, which may or may not have anything to do with the way things really are. In this regard civilization trumps nature, and the so-called real world becomes the one that we've created and not what happens in nature.

Hence the madness of civilization and everything that goes with it. The mind is a powerful thing, indeed.

In his book, *The Selfish Gene*, Richard Dawkins argues that, "We, and all other animals, are machines created by our genes." While most of his critics focus on the word "selfish," which is not only in the title but permeates this work, I see his use of the word "machine" as a much greater concern. Dawkins is quite impressed with evolution, and rightly so. It is the most powerful force in nature. "Why did the ancient replicators club together to make, and reside in, lumbering robots," Dawkins wonders, "And why are those robots – individual bodies, you and me – so large and so complicated?" In his enthusiasm for evolution, Dawkins reduces all living creatures to machines. "Lumbering robots" is an altogether mechanistic image, stemming from a strictly materialistic worldview in which things are perceived as merely the sum of their parts. But this worldview has little or nothing to do with the marvel of evolution. It is more the consequence of being all too civilized.

If it is true that nothing in nature is more than the sum of its parts, then what we make from these parts is as real as anything else. Here Dawkins is preaching to a choir of robots, to machines blessed with artificial intelligence, as well as those carbon life forms quite comfortable with becoming cogs in a great global system. No doubt cyborgs – those ambiguous science fiction contrivances, half human and half machine – would also agree wholeheartedly with Dawkins. To them all this blather about wildness and being human is utter nonsense. Being human, all these mechanistic creatures would agree, is a matter of opinion and wildness has nothing to do with it.

So there it is. In the end we will *think* ourselves out of existence, making our so-called humanity what we imagine it to be instead of what it is by nature. A special kind of ethic is essential for making this happen, of course. Convince enough people that being mechanistic is the ultimate good, and humankind (or what's left of it) will turn into machines. And why not? Without wildness as a reference point, being human can be whatever we imagine it to be. More importantly, being human won't matter. In due time, humanity will become irrelevant in a vast, self-sustaining global system that exists only to perpetuate itself – the ultimate bureaucracy, a mockery of nature. Then it'll be all about Dawkins' machines, organic or otherwise, simply acquiring more power over other machines.

I believe, as some others do, that social stratification, grotesque inequalities and the unnecessary limitations that accompany all forms of civilization are functions of power – namely, the power of a few over the many. This being the case, then the fix would seem to be a simple one: give power back to the people and everything will be right with the world. But the fundamental problem that plagues humankind runs deeper than that. Much deeper. All human successes can be traced back to abstract thinking, as can all our failures. We can imagine anything and, given enough power, those imaginations can become laws regardless of the realities of the natural world. Hence the madness of civilization. To fix this, we have to get real, meaning we have to get back in touch with nature. To be more specific, we have to get back in touch with our own wild nature. For any given individual, this isn't too hard to do. But for society at large, it will be a monumental task, especially when the mostly tame people in it are confused about what nature, humanity and wildness are in the first place.

The problem of civilization is reflected in the minds of each and every one of us. In other words, the problem is fundamentally an *interior* one. What is the mind but a mirror of the world in which it finds itself? The contemporary writer Diane Ackerman asks a more pertinent question: "When we spend most of our lives indoors, what becomes of our own wilderness?" There is no point preserving wild places if people never have any desire to go there. The first and most important wilderness that we need to protect is the one within. This we can't do if we are always surrounded by four walls, and staring into an electronic devices. It's a vicious circle. If future generations spend no time at all in wild places, they will be unable to even imagine wildness, much less feel it stirring within. One has to venture out and away from the glowing screen and see the world as it really is. Otherwise natural reality becomes unimaginable.

Sorry Mr. Dawkins, my dog is not a robot. Neither am I. The difference between my dog and me is that I can think this and say this. My dog, on the other hand, simply goes about the business of being a dog. In that regard, she remains fully ensconced in nature despite her domestication, despite all the limitations that I as a domesticating force have imposed upon her. In this regard, she is wilder, freer than I am, unencumbered by any thought of robot-ness. But I struggle with robot-ness, forcefully asserting my humanity, all too aware that other people like me have already surrendered their humanity to this notion or are damned close to doing so. To such people I think a week alone in a wild place would provide a much-needed sense of perspective. Perhaps then the reality of the natural world would undermine their robot-ness. Or perhaps not. More troubling than this possibility is the fact that not everyone could have such an experience even if they wanted it. There aren't enough wild places left on this planet to accommodate billions of people trying to reconnect with natural reality. In that regard, we are already well down the road towards a world beyond human nature.

18. Naturally Human

I am a wild man. I am a creature of the earth before I am a member of society. I am also civilized, yes, but recognize no law, principle or belief system that separates me from the rest of nature. I am wild at heart, fully aware that being human means being a part of the natural world. Therein lies my ultimate loyalty, transcending any sense of duty that I feel to my community, the nation in which I live, or to the all-encompassing global civilization. Wildness is not a distant or idealized concept to me. It is my frame of mind, the way my body functions, the way I live my life despite the myriad constrictions imposed upon me by society. I cannot speak for all humankind, but this much I know about myself: without wild places in which to roam, I would cease to exist.

All I can say with certainty, beyond my subjective understanding of the world and myself, is that humankind arose from nature and remains a part of it. As Gary Snyder wrote in *The Practice of the Wild*: "Nature is not a place to visit, it is *home*." It is where we are from, where we live, and where we belong. We can, of course, destroy this home. Perhaps someday we may even be able to leave it. We possess the technology to radically alter it, and in the distant future we just might create an entirely artificial world from it. But is that what we really want? More to the point, if we do so, will we still be human in any meaningful sense of the word?

The home planet. We undervalue it at our peril. There are those among us who get all starry-eyed when they imagine humankind going to Mars, colonizing it, then venturing deeper and deeper into the universe. That is their version of the human spirit – the endless quest for new worlds, the conquest of nature, and victory over all obstacles! To them the home planet is a rather mundane place, and living in harmony with nature here and now is not something worthy of our best efforts. They talk about an asteroid hitting this planet and destroying our world as if that's a good argument for abandoning it. But I am not a Martian. I'm an Earthling and *this* planet, *this* world, is my home pure and simple. And when it dies, my kind – humankind, that is – will die with it. I am not interested in helping some allegedly superhuman species of hominid spread across the galaxy in the distant future. Nor am I interested in living in a completely artificial world like a spaceship, an underground bunker, or the equivalent of that built on some other planet. I live here on Earth, a world all green and blue and fecund, and value it more than any utopian world that those enamored by technology can imagine.

We need the resources of this planet in order to survive. We need clean water to drink, soil in which to grow food, the wood, stone and other materials of it to build homes and roads, and so on. We are as dependent upon nature's resources now as we have ever been. But we need to be smart about how we utilize those resources. With our population pressing onto eight billion now, we need to be really smart about what we do and don't do. Otherwise we will progress into a Malthusian nightmare where the demand for resources greatly exceeds the supply. Worse yet, we will utilize those natural resources to the point where they are no longer recoverable. Then what will happen to us?

It's all a matter of values – what we value and what don't value. Whatever plan we come up with to fuel the engine of global civilization, it has to be something that works beyond the next generation or two. It has to be a long-term plan. As the agriculturalist Wendell Berry wrote: "The goal is a harmony between the human economy and nature that will preserve both nature and humanity, and this is a traditional goal." It is traditional in the sense that no sapient creature ever destroys the wellspring of its livelihood. If we truly value the well being of our species as a whole, then we will take good care of our home planet.

The problem of civilization, the one that affects all of humankind now that civilization is globalizing, is the profound disconnect between the world we have created for ourselves and the reality of nature. Consequently, we are subject to the madness of civilization – to infinitely complex systems, dysfunctional bureaucracies, legal and moral absurdities, grotesque inequalities, widespread misinformation, a frenzied pace of life, unnecessary stress, and traditional values so distorted that they have become meaningless. Those who materially benefit from this mess perpetuate it, of course, along with those who believe that the violence inherent in this arrangement is a natural thing. Some people, like that 17th century cynic Thomas Hobbes, tell us that it's a dog-eat-dog world, as if what we do to each other within the context of civilization is somehow natural, but that couldn't be further from the truth. Nature has nothing to do with it. In fact, if we were more in touch with the rhythms of nature, the world we have created wouldn't be such a mess. The madness of civilization isn't nature's fault. We have no one to blame but ourselves.

In 1948, shortly after the horrors of the Second World War, the General Assembly of the newly formed United Nations passed Resolution 217A: The Universal Declaration of Human Rights. Its 30 Articles promote human freedom and well being, addressing most if not all of the fundamental evils that result from the clash of cultures, the abuse of power, and the shortcomings of civilization in general. If all nations practiced what is preached in that document, we would be well on our way towards promoting the best of humanity while checking the worst of it. Curiously enough, there is nothing in that document that a wild man like myself finds objectionable. The rights declared there are inalienable ones – ones that we all possess naturally as human beings. The fact that they have to be declared by an international assembly just goes to show how widespread the violations of our natural freedoms really are. The civilizations that we have created to date have all failed us. Can a *global* civilization do any better?

We are human by nature, yet nature itself is something that we do not respect. Not really. We talk about the balance of nature and our role in that as if nature is something static and manageable. We think we can control it, as if nature is nothing more than a great big machine. We grossly underestimate nature's power, its efficacy. In our incredible hubris, we look upon the whole universe and say it is all for us. But a cosmic event will wipe us out someday. We will not end nature; it will end us. Then nature will go on. If we as sapient creatures are serious about surviving our collective stupidity until that cosmic event happens, then we had better start taking the dynamics of nature seriously.

Whenever I venture alone into a truly wild place, I soon discover that I'm not the one calling the shots, nature is. Then I change my behavior accordingly. That is how I survived the Alaskan bush, and how I have managed to return home in one piece from all of my wilderness excursions. But eventually nature will get the best of me, either deep in the woods or more likely on my deathbed here in the developed lowlands. Nature always wins. I, *Homo sapiens*, am an incredibly sapient creature, but not nearly as sapient as I think I am. Death is the one thing I cannot overcome. But collectively speaking, we could stay alive and thrive in this world for eons, if we start acting like the sapient creatures that we are supposed to be.

We are human by nature yet there is something about nature that I, as a civilized man, cannot fully comprehend. No matter how much time I spend in the wild, something about it remains just a little alien to me. This is not just a personal problem. It is the fundamental problem of civilization as a whole and everyone in it. This sense of alienation is not healthy. As the writer John Fowles said, "As long as nature is seen as in some way outside us, frontiered and foreign, *separate*, it is lost both to us and in us." How can we fix this?

I do not pretend to have the answers to all the problems that plague humankind, nor can I say with absolute certainty what it means to be human. I have no crystal ball either, so I hesitate making any specific statements about the future of humanity or our home planet. But I do know that I am energized by the wild, and find myself relating to it more and more with each passing day. I also know that I am not alone in this, and suspect that my visceral response to wildness is something universal, something that comes with being human.

I'm well aware that calling myself both a wild man and a civilized man seems rather contradictory, but I stand by it. Most people assume that something dramatic happened to us at the beginning of civilization – something that makes us more human than our distant, hunting and gathering ancestors. But I am convinced that no such dramatic event ever took place, and that the remnant tribes of hunter-gatherers still alive today are no less human than I am. Our humanity runs deep into the natural world. There is wildness in us all that the circumstances we are born into cannot change. Being civilized diminishes my wildness, no doubt, but it does not eliminate it. On every outing I take alone into deep woods, I grow a little more feral. And it is more likely that I may never return from one of these outings than it is that I will give up being wild.

Wildness is, after all, a part of me. Wild and free. That is what it feels like to be fully human, *naturally* human. The manic life that I live here in the developed lowlands, well, this is something else altogether.

Notes

Quote Page

"I wish to speak a word for Nature…" Henry David Thoreau, "Walking" essay taken from *Excursions*, a reprint of his shorter works (Corinth Books, 1962), p. 161.

Chapter 2 – The Human Conundrum

"All moral doctrines…" Mary Midgley, *Beast and Man: The Roots of Human Nature* (Cornell University Press, 1978), p. 166.

"The special sciences that deal with man…" Max Scheler, *Man's Place in Nature* (Farrar, Straus and Cudahy, 1962), p. 6.

"A man who has become conscious…" Albert Camus, *The Myth of Sisyphus and Other Essays* (Random House, Vintage Books, 1955), p. 24.

"Man is a stream…" Ralph Waldo Emerson, from his essay "The Over-Soul," found in *Emerson's Essays* (Thomas Y. Crowell, Apollo Edition, 1961), p. 189.

Chapter 3 – Wild, Not Wild

"Animal is a word…" Jacques Derrida, *The Animal That Therefore I Am* (Fordham University Press, 2008), p. 32.

"Biological determinism…must be incorporated…" Bronislaw Malinowski, *A Scientific Theory of Culture and Other Essays* (Oxford University Press, 1960), p. 79.

"No, it is bone of our bone…" Ralph Waldo Emerson, *Natural History of Intellect and Other Papers* (Houghton Mifflin, Centenary Edition, 1904), p. 165.

"In our most serious moments…" Paul Gruchow, *The Necessity of Empty Places* (Milkweed Editions, 1999), p. 169.

"Know thyself." A common phrase, sometimes attributed to the ancient Greek philosopher Socrates, supposedly inscribed on the wall of the forecourt of the Temple of Apollo at Delphi.

"No man ever looks…" Ruth Benedict, *Patterns of Culture* (Routledge & Kegan Paul Ltd, 1971 reprint), p. 2.

Chapter 4 – What is Nature?

"Who are we, and what is Nature…" Ralph Waldo Emerson, *Natural History of Intellect and Other Papers*, p. 16.

"Do we dare think…" Max Oelschlaeger, *The Idea of Wilderness* (Yale University Press, 1991), p. 350.

"Now the empire of man…" Francis Bacon, *Novum Organum*, quoted by Clarence J. Glacken in *Traces on the Rhodian Shore* (University of California Press, 1967), p. 473.

Chapter 6 – Defining the Human

"…Of every man against every man" and "…solitary, poor, nasty, brutish and short" Thomas Hobbes, *Leviathan, Parts I and II* (Bobbs-Merrill, 1958, 13th printing), p. 106-107.

"Compassion is a natural feeling…." Jean-Jacques Rousseau, *Discourse on Inequality*, translated by G. D. H. Cole. Available online as a PDF provided by the American University of Beirut (AUB), p. 20.

"The general will is always right…" Jean-Jacques Rousseau, *Of the Social Contract* (King's Court Communications, 1978), p. 18.

"Man is a part of the universe…" John Burroughs, *Accepting the Universe* (Fredonia Books, 2001 reprint), p. 45.

"The theory of human nature that prevails…" Charles J. Lumsden and Edward O. Wilson, *Promethean Fire: Reflections on the Origin of Mind* (Harvard University Press, 1983), p. 85.

"Those naturalists who admit…" Charles Darwin, *The Descent of Man, and Selection in Relation to Sex*, excerpted in *The Portable Darwin*, edited by Duncan M. Porter and Peter W. Graham (Penguin Books, 1993), p. 335.

Chapter 7 – Hominids

"The question of questions for mankind…" Thomas H. Huxley, *Evidence as to Man's Place in Nature* (D. Appleton and Company, 1863), p. 71. Online at archive.org.

"The difference in mind…" Charles Darwin, *The Portable Darwin*, p. 330.

"There is a great deal in chimpanzee social relations…" Jane Goodall, *In the Shadow of Man* (Houghton Mifflin, 1988, revised edition), p. 129-30.

"Human prehistory evidently took a major turn…" Richard Leakey, *The Origin of Humankind* (Basic Books, 1994), p. xiv (preface).

"The 'missing link' is an artificial construct…" Alan Walker and Pat Shipman, *The Wisdom of the Bones* (Alfred A. Knopf, 1996), p. 259-60.

"This physical body of ours…" Joseph Campbell, *The Flight of the Wild Gander* (Regnery/Gateway, 1979), p. 145.

"There is now a consensus that the ultimate roots…" F. Clark Howell's contribution to *Origins of Anatomically Modern Humans*, edited by Matthew H. Nitecki and Doris V. Nitecki (Plenum Press, 1994), p. 302.

'Work on mtDNA in modern humans…" Rebecca Cann's contribution to *Origins of Anatomically Modern Humans*, p. 137.

"The animality of man…" Abraham J. Heschel, *Who Is Man?* (Stanford University Press, 1965), p. 3.

Chapter 8 – The Emergence of Fully Human Beings

"By culture I mean the transfer…" John T. Bonner, *The Evolution of Culture in Animals* (Princeton University Press, 1989), p. 9.

"Some of the known differences in coding…" Christopher Stringer, "What Makes a Modern Human" in the journal *Nature*, 3 May 2012, volume 485, p. 35. Available online as a PDF by Researchgate.net.

"Virtually everyone agrees…" Richard G. Klein with Blake Edgar, *The Dawn of Human Culture* (John Wiley & Sons, 2002), p. 209.

"The Neanderthals probably went out…" Christopher Stringer, quoted by James Shreeve in *The Neandertal Enigma: Solving the Mystery of Modern Human Origins* (William Morrow and Company, 1995), p. 338.

"As evidence for rapid technological changes…" Ofer Bar-Yosef, "The Upper Paleolithic Revolution" in the *Annual Review of Anthropology*, 2002, volume 31, p. 369.

"The last key neural change…" Richard Klein, *The Dawn of Human Culture*, p. 271.

"Language is a force for change…" Brian Fagan, *Cro-Magnon* (Bloomsbury Press, 2011), p. 80.

"Simple logic says there can be no learning...." Steven Pinker, *The Blank Slate: The Modern Denial of Human Nature* (Viking Penguin, 2002)), p. 101.

"Many species communicate..."Alan Barnard, *Genesis of Symbolic Thought* (Cambridge University Press, 2012), p. 3.

"Symbolization is the essential act of mind..." Suzanne K. Langer, *Philosophy in a New Key* (Harvard University Press, 1957, 3rd Edition), p. 41.

"Humanity in the beginning lacks..." Emile Durkheim and Marcel Mauss, *Primitive Classification* (University of Chicago Press, 1963), p. 7.

"The first logical categories..." Emile Durkheim and Marcel Mauss, *Primitive Classification*, p. 82.

"Believing, with Max Weber, that man is an animal suspended in webs of significance he himself has spun, I take culture as those webs..." Clifford Geertz, *The Interpretation of Cultures* (Basic Books, 1973), p. 5.

"Culture is public because meaning is." Clifford Geertz, *The Interpretation of Cultures*, p. 12.

"There is almost certainly a cultural continuity..." Alan Barnard, *Genesis of Symbolic Thought*, p. 32.

"Breuil believed that art began..." Gregory Curtis, *The Cave Painters* (Anchor books, 2007), p. 76.

"It is this feeling which..." Rudolf Otto, *The Idea of the Holy* (Oxford University Press, 1958), p. 14.

Chapter 10 – Becoming Civilized

"A person whose behavior…" Leslie A. White, *The Evolution of Culture: The Development of Civilization to the Fall of Rome* (McGraw-Hill, 1959), p. 228.

"Christine Hastorf, an archaeologist from Berkeley, California, stresses the significance of 'plant nurturing' in understanding the earliest stages of plant domestication." Steven Mithen, *After the Ice: A Global Human History, 20,000-5,000 BC* (Harvard University Press, 2004), p. 35.

"The sedentary hunter-gatherers…" Steven Mithen, *After the Ice*, p. 44.

"In light of the permanence of the settlements…" Steven Mithen, *After the Ice*, p. 36.

"History repeated itself…" Steven Mithen, *After the Ice*, p. 57.

"Farmers find themselves in a vicious spiral…" Colin Tudge, *Neanderthals, Bandits and Farmers: How Agriculture Really Began* (Yale University Press, 1999), p. 33.

"We are only about…" Annie Dillard, *For the Time Being* (Vintage Books, 1999), p. 119.

Chapter 11 – The March of Civilization

"Simple cultures normally belong to small societies…" Elman R. Service, *Origins of the State and Civilization: The Process of Cultural Evolution* (Norton, 1975), p. 306.

"The creation and extension of the authority bureaucracy…" Elman R. Service, *Origins of the Sate and Civilization*, p. 285.

"Social organization was transformed…" Leslie A. White, *The Evolution of Culture*, p. 281.

"The peoples of areas with a head start…" Jared Diamond, *Guns, Germs, and Steel: The Fates of Human Societies* (Norton, 1999), p. 103.

"Of fifty-nine people buried in the graveyard…" Steven Mithen, *After the Ice*, p. 452.

"There is nothing in the evidence so far unearthed…" Walter A. Fairservis, Jr., *The Threshold of Civilization: An Experiment in Prehistory* (Charles Scribner's Sons, 1975), p. 199.

"If we have become a debt society…" David Graeber, *Debt: The First 5,000 Years* (Melville House, 2014), p. 164.

"Only with the transition to societies organized…" Jürgen Habermas, *Communication and the Evolution of Society* (Beacon Press, 1979), p. 104.

"The chief problem of man…" Abraham J. Heschel, *Who Is Man?*, p. 10.

Chapter 12 – Savage or Civilized?

"Physical apishness can explain…" Stephen Jay Gould, *The Mismeasure of Man* (Norton, 1993 reissue), p. 124-125.

"We live in a more subtle century…" Stephen Jay Gould, *The Mismeaure of Man*, p. 143.

"The natural assumption is…" Nicholas Wade, *Before the Dawn: Recovering the Lost History of Our Ancestors* (Penguin Press, 2006), p. 103.

"Universal kinship…" Alan Barnard, *Genesis of Symbolic Thought*, p. 56.

"Natural humanity…" Alan Barnard, *Genesis of Symbolic Thought*, p. 121.

"Everything we had suspected..." Bernard-Henri Lévy, *War, Evil, and the End of History* (Melville House, 2004), p. 298.

Chapter 13 – The Tonic of Wilderness

"From the forest and wilderness come..." Henry David Thoreau, "Walking" essay in *Excursions*, p. 185.

"In Wildness is the preservation of the World..." Henry David Thoreau, "Walking" essay in *Excursions*, p. 185.

"The clearest way into the Universe..." John Muir, *The Wilderness World of John Muir*, edited by Edwin Way Teale (Houghton Mifflin, 1954, 12th printing), p. 312.

"In the wilderness I am reminded..." Holmes Rolston III, *Philosophy Gone Wild: Essays in Environmental Ethics* (Prometheus Books, 1986), p. 123.

"Wilderness is a bizarre place..." Homes Rolston III, *Philosophy Gone Wild*, p. 137.

"Far from being the one place on earth..." William Cronin, "The Trouble with Wilderness, or, Getting Back to the Wrong Nature," an essay taken from *Uncommon Ground: Rethinking the Human Place in Nature* (Norton, 1995) p. 69. PDF available online at williamcronon.net.

"It is not often that we can shed..." John Hay, *The Immortal Wilderness* (Norton, 1987), p. 74.

Chapter 15 – Global Civilization

"Men of today seem to feel..." Simone de Beauvoir, *The Ethics of Ambiguity* (The Citadel Press, 1972, 6th printing), p. 8-9.

"Homo sapiens, the only creature endowed..." Henri Bergson, *The Two Sources of Morality and Religion* (Doubleday Anchor Books, 1956), p. 102.

"As soon as Power is conceived..." Bertrand de Jouvenel, *On Power: Its Nature and the History of Its Growth* (Beacon Press, 1969, 3rd printing), p. 124.

"What is meant by calling man fallible?" Paul Ricoeur, *Fallible Man: Philosophy of the Will* (Henry Regnery Company, 1967, 2nd printing), p. 205.

Chapter 16 – Wildness, Freedom and Being Human

"Of what avail are forty freedoms..." Aldo Leopold, *A Sand County Almanac and Sketches Here and There* (Oxford University Press, 1982), p. 149.

"You can chain me, you can torture me..." Quote by Mahatma Gandhi found at bbc.co.uk/worldservice/learningenglish/ movingwords/quotefeature/gandhi.shtml. Also displayed at dozens of other websites and reprinted in books of quotations.

"Man was designed for very small societies..." Henri Bergson, *The Two Sources of Morality and Religion*, p. 275.

"While their specific positions on relativism in anthropology or literacy in modern society may not accord, Goody, Lévi-Strauss and Sperber all agree. 'Untamed thought' is prevalent in the human condition..." Alan Barnard, *Genesis of Symbolic Thought*, p. 127.

Chapter 17 – Beyond Human Nature

"This outward projection of attention..." Loren Eiseley, *The Firmament of Time* (University of Nebraska Press, 1999), p. 134-135.

"We, and all other animals, are machines..." Richard Dawkins, *The Selfish Gene* (Oxford University Press, 2006), p. 2.

"Why did the ancient replicators..." Richard Dawkins, *The Selfish Gene*, p. 237.

"When we spend most of our lives indoors..." Diane Ackerman, *Deep Play* (Vintage Books, 1999), p. 156.

Chapter 18 – Naturally Human

"Nature is not a place to visit..." Gary Snyder, *The Practice of the Wild* (North Point Press, 1990), p. 7.

"The goal is a harmony..." Wendell Berry, *What Are People For?* (North Point Press, 1990), p. 107.

"As long as nature is seen as in some way outside us..." John Fowles, *The Tree* (The Ecco Press, 1983), p. 78.

About the Author

Walt McLaughlin holds a degree in philosophy but insists that his thoughts regarding the relationship between nature and humankind have arisen largely from his backcountry experiences. He has been wondering, wandering and writing for over 40 years. He has fifteen books in print, including a narrative about his immersion in the Alaskan bush, *Arguing with the Wind*, another about backpacking through the Adirondacks, *The Allure of Deep Woods*, and a collection of essays, *Cultivating the Wildness Within*. He is also the force behind a small press called Wood Thrush Books, and has selected and published the works of Ralph Waldo Emerson and other 19th Century nature writers as well as contemporary ones. He lives in Swanton, Vermont with his wife, Judy.

For more information about Walt's books, visit the WTB website: **www.woodthrushbooks.com**

Go to **www.facebook.com\WaltMcLaughlin** to check out his Facebook page, or read his regularly posted blogs at **woodswanderer.com**. You can also find his essays and short narratives at **medium.com**.

www.ingramcontent.com/pod-product-compliance
Lightning Source LLC
Chambersburg PA
CBHW030108300326
41934CB00034B/662